MY FORMBY

*

RECOLLECTIONS OF VILLAGE LIFE

by
JOAN A. RIMMER

Illustrations by Muriel Sibley

To the memory of my parents

ISBN 0 903348 14 4

Published and produced in Great Britain by
Print Origination (NW) Limited
Formby Industrial Estate
Formby, Liverpool L37 8EG
Printed in Great Britain by Bell and Bain Ltd., Glasgow

ACKNOWLEDGEMENTS

I wish to thank everyone who has helped me in making this book possible, especially the following who so willingly lent me photographs and other material for publication: the late Mrs Mary Rimmer, Mrs Mary Norris, Mrs Margaret Rimmer, Miss Margaret Rimmer, Mrs Joan Castle, Mrs Anne Rothwell, Mr and Mrs Harry Ashcroft, Mr and Mrs Colin Corless, Mrs Maud Kays, Mrs Jean Raistrick, Mrs Irene Postlethwaite, Mr Derek Postlethwaite, Mrs Gabrielle Hutchinson, Mr Wilf Wright, and of course Mrs Muriel Sibley whose continuing generosity is so greatly appreciated. Also the following for their invaluable memory jogging, advice, and interest: Miss Marjorie Strong, Mr Howard Corless, Mrs Audrey Wright, Mr Vernon Thomas, Mrs Joan Brown, Mr John Young, Mrs Joyce Patten, and Mr Paul Watson. I am more than grateful to each and every one of them.

FOREWORD

In 1987 when my first collection of poems was published I little knew of the enormous interest they would generate, and that such simple verses of everyday events and people would prove so popular. Within weeks 2,000 copies had sped around Formby and across the world. The following year my second publication appeared and the whole nostalgia scene was in full swing. It seemed that everyone had an insatiable yearning for the past—for a way of life that had somehow drifted into oblivion. Progress had swept us all along unawares and the vast changes around us had been a gradual process, slightly bewildering, mildly regrettable, but apathetically accepted as inevitable until suddenly one tiny book of poems seemed to stop us all in our tracks.

We are not unique. There are countless 'Formbys' up and down the land whose small communities have been swallowed up or taken over. For those like myself who remember it all there must be regrets for what we have lost and for our impotence in allowing it all to happen. For newcomers there is a curiosity of how it used to be and an incredulity of such change. For all of us there should be interest and a little concern. It has happened. We cannot go back. But we can look back and we can remember. For every poem I have written there are many stories some of which I would like to share with you in recalling the village I loved so dearly. As a conclusion to the book both volumes of my poems, originally published under the titles FORMBY MEMORIES and MORE FORMBY MEMORIES and now out of print again, have by request been added, together with a further selection, as a relevant part of the Formby story. I hope that a younger generation may also find the book interesting. My thanks go to all the people of Formby with whom I grew up and lived amongst. They made the story. All I have done is to tell it in the way I remember it.

MY FORMBY

Formby was a magical place when I was a child. Looking
back to those war-time days it is difficult to envisage that
childhood village when looking at Formby today. This trip
down memory lane will recall the characters and places
which were the cornerstones of life here in those not too far
off days which could be a million years ago.

I do not want to dwell too much on my ancestry but it
does seem relevant to use some space in establishing where I
fit into the story and give a little of my background. My
parents, like their parents, etc., were sandgrounders. My
mother's family were staunchly Roman Catholic, and it was
viewed with horror by them all when my mother committed
the mortal sin of marrying my father, an equally devout
Protestant, at St Michael's Church, Altcar on 21st October
1929. The rift continued until some six years later when their
first and only children, my twin brother and I, were born on
29th April 1935 and we seemed to some extent to heal the
breach in the relationship.

Religious intolerance at that time was very intense in
Formby and it was only in later years I realised how very
courageous my mother had been in defying her mother
and how very much she must have cared for my father
to do so. A very formidable lady was my grandmother!
My grandmother's maiden name was Alice Formby. She
came from a farming family and on leaving Our Lady's

5

School became a teacher there until her marriage to Thomas Ashcroft. She had five surviving children and my mother, Annie, being the eldest was expected to bear much of the household responsibilities.

My grandfather died before I was born, but quite early in his married life had suffered a severe accident in which he lost his leg. Times were hard and my grandmother and all the children worked tirelessly to make a living. As the family grew up my grandmother became the proprietress of the local fish and chip shop, a venture viewed with great disdain by other branches of the family, where she worked extremely hard, with her two daughters, my mother and my aunt Edith, as almost unpaid slaves. She also showed great enterprise and business acumen by dabbling in property deals and moving from house to house quite frequently, borrowing money to do so—something quite extraordinary in those days for a woman with a disabled husband, a large family and no capital.

My mother's entire life seemed to consist of hard work. On leaving school, unlike most working-class girls who went into service, she worked in the office of MacSymon's grocery store in Formby Village learning the rudiments of book-keeping and accounts. She moved from there to Bobby's, a high class department store in Lord Street, Southport (much later to become Debenham's) starting off as the office junior and quickly climbing the ladder to eventually take charge of the accounts department. Again unlike the norm for those times she continued working after her marriage staying with Bobby's for thirteen happy years and leaving them only two months before the birth of my twin brother and myself. From then onwards she worked indefatigably for my grandmother at the chip shop lifting and carrying great sacks of potatoes, 'eyeing' potatoes by hand in icy buckets of water as well as looking after us all at home. The early death of my father necessitated her finding a job and this was when she joined the counter staff of Rimmer's fruit and vegetable shop (no relation) on the corner of the village, only leaving them to nurse her mother through her final illness. After the death of my grandmother she went back to work again this time at

Ewing's cake shop in the village where she stayed until retiring in her 60's. For the remainder of her life she played an active part in the village community establishing, along with her namesake Councillor Jimmy Rimmer's wife, the weekly whist drives at the Luncheon Club, and continuing in office with the Women's Gas Federation, of which she was a founder member, until ill health forced her resignation. She was very kind, generous, and wise. She was also my best friend. She died a few days after her 83rd birthday in January 1987.

My mother   My father

My father came from Great Altcar, though the family were originally from Formby. I have a family tree dating back to 1640 on my father's side and it gives me pleasure to see that one of his forbears, Dr. James Longton, was the first doctor to practise medicine in Southport. It would appear that somewhere along the line the family slid rapidly down the social scale when probably my great grandfather appeared

on the scene. This is only supposition, but from being
landowners and gentry there was obviously some fall from
grace as my grandfather, Robert Rimmer, who I remember so vividly and was the salt of the earth, could never
have been described as gentry! He was a grand old chap—
very forthright and down-to-earth, but like so many country
people unrefined and uneducated. He was a farm worker and
a genius with cattle and crops, always winning with his prize
cows at the annual Formby Flower Show.

My grandmother was a quiet, gentle and lovely lady
who bore him a daughter and four sons. Polly, the eldest,
worked all her life at the Formby Golf Club and was loved
and respected by all, from the staff to the members and
guests including the then Prince of Wales, later the Duke of
Windsor. My brother and I adored her and spent countless
happy hours at the Golf Club in a world far removed from
our own. The four sons were all fine strapping young men
and all tragically and unaccountably died in their 40's and
50's leaving their parents to mourn them. My father, Richard,
was 51 when he died, a tragic loss to us and to the many
people who loved him. He was a kind, gentle and happy
man—a true gentleman in every sense of the word, and to
this day I have never heard anyone speak ill of him. My
grandfather outlived all his family and died in his 80's and
was laid to rest alongside them all in Altcar churchyard.

That then is a potted background to my family. What
follows is my life in the most idyllic of settings—the Formby
of my childhood.

My earliest recollections are of the outbreak of war when I
was just four years of age. My brother, Derek, and I were
playing along our side path when my mother rushed out and
brought us in telling us that war had started. I think I
vaguely expected bombs to fall and guns to fire. Nothing
happened at all.

We started school at Holy Trinity in 1940 still unaffected by
the war, and those years at that tiny school were probably
amongst the happiest of my life. Formby's population was
around 7,000 though evacuees were beginning to arrive from

The Post Office and Holy Trinity School

Liverpool. We country children were a bit afraid of these streetwise kids with their strange accents who seemed so much tougher than we who had led such sheltered lives, but like children the world over we all mixed in together and life was fun.

I remember clearly the day I started school. My brother and I stood hand in hand inside the classroom door. My mother left us, and my brother immediately fled from the classroom to follow and find her, leaving me next to another small boy, now a successful tradesman in Formby, whose mother had also just departed leaving him in the classroom. He, obviously very frightened by his new surroundings, promptly wet the floor. I stood silently in total perplexity at the strange behaviour of these two boys.

We had just three classrooms and three teachers at Holy Trinity. Miss Reily, the headmistress, Miss Culshaw, the infant teacher, and Miss Heaton. Miss Heaton was everything the other two were not. A local girl, young, attractive, sang in the church choir, and played the piano. We would all stand around her piano and sing our hearts out as she accompanied us. The school had a small variety of musical instruments and when we had music lessons I always longed for the tambourine and always got the triangle. I still remember the bitter disappointment of producing a pathetic ping from the instrument when I so desperately wanted to be responsible for a gigantic sound. The boys maybe fared less well with Miss Heaton. She was strict, as were all our teachers, and used the ruler mercilessly on those boys who misbehaved, but she only ever needed to use it once. We all loved her and would do anything to please her and when she married the curate from our church, the Rev. Fred Bussby, it seemed a fairy tale come true.

Miss Culshaw was quiet and patient and seemed rather in awe of Miss Reily. She drove a car which for a woman in those days was quite unusual. She had a difficult job in starting off the basic education of us all. Her class-room had a big fireplace with a roaring fire blazing, a rocking horse in the corner, and charts around the walls with a large number on each followed by the appropriate number of spots to indicate that number. To make a number 5 we were instructed to make the boiler, then the chimney and then the smoke! We were all relentlessly rehearsed in our 'times' tables—something I have never forgotten and in the age of the calculator might seem totally unnecessary but to me, and no doubt all my contemporaries, is a priceless asset. Reading, writing and arithmetic were the essentials.

Miss Reily was the very masculine head of the school, completely unconcerned with her appearance and claiming never to use a mirror. She wore the same hat throughout her entire working life. She was tall and angular with enormous bony hands and feet, and when peering at the classroom clock seemed to develop a grimacing squint. Miss Reily instilled terror into our very souls with her tremendous bellow, but although she was feared she was also respected, and as we grew older held in great affection by many. Her christian kindness to those children in any way under-privileged was illustrated in many ways and especially in her generosity in having children to stay at her home in Southport for short holidays. She read us enchanting stories and poems. She took us on nature walks where we identified so many different wild flowers, trees, and birds. Great emphasis was laid on neatness and correct spelling, and there was a definite yet unobtrusive religious background to our education with prayers and hymns being held every morning and evening. Our vicar, Canon Dawson, was a familiar figure to us all and every Christmas would come into the school and give each child a silver threepenny bit.

Miss Reily's home was in Southport, but during the war years when transport wasn't always reliable she lodged at Raby Bank, a large detached house owned by Mrs. Rennie on the corner of Elbow Lane and Cropton Road (now replaced by a modern house). Her lunch (or rather dinner as we called

The Village cottages of Mawdsleys and Wainds

it), in the days before school meals, was cooked for her by Mrs. Waind, an old lady who lived in one of the nearby cottages in the Village, and at 12 noon two children would be sent to collect the meal. On one occasion, a Pancake Tuesday in fact, as the girls were carrying the dinner to the school a dog jumped up and ate the pancake. In fear and trepidation the empty plate was produced. It seemed such a feeble excuse to say a dog had eaten the pancake, but presumably for that very reason Miss Reily accepted the explanation. In later years and especially towards the end of her teaching career Miss Reily mellowed considerably and the familiar sight of her striding figure accompanied by countless children all vying for the distinction of carrying her case to and from the station was an indication of the feelings of her young charges.

All our teachers were strict disciplinarians and there were probably times when we hated them—or thought we did! We all knew without any doubt the fate which would befall us if we misbehaved, and most of us had the good sense to avoid such punishment. Whether we did so or not their treatment of us left no emotional scars in later years, and in fact our teachers were held in great affection and remembered with gratitude for their care and dedication.

The school itself was a solid red brick building at the end of the Village next to the bank and the post office. The tiny cloakroom was immediately inside the entrance with the largest classroom beyond the cloakroom. A partition divided that classroom from the smaller one at the far end of the school from which we entered the playground. The infants' classroom was on the right of the school. The playground was minute with all the toilets situated across the yard, and come rain, hail, or snow the only way to reach them was by running through the puddles to the freezing compartments at the other side. We never lingered long. The playground was so tiny that when the weather was suitable we were all taken in a long crocodile to Duke Street Park for games, or football in the case of the boys. If the weather was bad we all filed into the parish hall for country dancing.

Being at school during the war meant carrying our gas masks with us every day. Mine was an ordinary model in a cardboard box which was slung across my shoulder, and how I envied those fortunate children who had Mickey Mouse gas masks. We were all expected to wear our gas masks on the days we were taken to the air raid shelter behind the

Beauford Hall as an emergency exercise, but as the horrible contraption almost caused me to suffocate I never did actually put mine properly on my face.

There was a little passage way through to the school entrance alongside the Village shops. Walking home through the Village we first passed McLardy's outfitters where Lizzie

The Village

Massam was the assistant and where her invalid sister could often be seen in her bath chair outside the door watching the comings and goings of the customers.

Lovelady's cake shop was next door and the smell of freshly baked bread from the bake-house wafted across our tiny playground. It was a real treat when we could afford a ha'penny to buy a crusty cob to eat on the way home. The windows of Lovelady's were covered with big brown blinds on Wednesday afternoons which was half day closing, and we children would all take turns to stand half way in the doorway raising one arm and leg to see our reflection in the window as though both arms and legs were being raised—a trick enjoyed by comedian Harry Worth on a very much later T.V. programme.

Next to Lovelady's were the two cottages of Ben Mawdsley and his sister Sally Postlethwaite and her family, and their neighbours, the Wainds. The huge pear tree in Mawdsley's garden was always laden with fruit, and flowers grew profusely. Golding's the cobblers came next, and then Wright's fruit and vegetable shop. Charlie Sole had a tiny shop where he sold and repaired clocks and watches, and Clinch's the cleaners was alongside with a public clock above their shop and where Rose Gallagher was in charge of our sartorial cleanliness.

Irwin's the grocers came next with Fred Stevens on the bacon slicer and Peter Thomas on the delivery van, then Clague's the chemists next to Inchboard's haberdashery and

Mr. Clague and Mr. Corless outside their pharmacy (now McDougall's)

Parker's haberdashery and hairdressers. These shops were protected by iron verandahs giving shelter on rainy days, and were ideal meeting places for our mothers to chat. Bill Swift's bike shop was next, across the entry, with the most jumbled mess of rusty articles covered in dust. The boys cat-called at old Bill who often lay in wait with a tin-can full of water, which we strongly suspected was his own, and pitched the lot over the nearest child.

Halstead's butchers was next door and then Ernie Bills' saddlery (he later moved down the Village next to the school). With so many farms in the village Mr. Bills had a thriving saddlery business and the wonderful smell of leather pervaded the shop as you entered. Apart from the obvious work on saddles and bridles he dealt in any type of leather work. As we grew older and became the proud possessors of school satchels they invariably needed repairing at the end of term and at the start of the long summer holidays. We always took them to Mr. Bills immediately we broke up school and always without fail at the end of the holidays we would still be pestering him for the return of the satchels. We never got them back until the day before returning to school which in Mr. Bills' opinion was just what we needed and quite soon enough! Mr Bills also had the important job of carrying out any repairs to the huge Union Jack flag which was displayed on the Council Offices flag pole.

The Food Office was next (on the site of the present Gas Showrooms) set back in a garden, with Freddy Norburn in charge and where our mothers queued up for our ration books. Everything from food to clothing was rationed, but despite the meagre rations we were very fortunate to be living in the country where most people grew their own vegetables, kept poultry, and knew how to acquire the odd hare or pheasant. We were particularly lucky having grandparents living in the farming community of Altcar and therefore there was no noticeable shortage of fresh vegetables, fruit, eggs, and when a pig was killed (by licence of course!), pork, bacon and the most delicious black puddings in the world. My grandmother was renowned for her home-made black puddings, and whenever a pig was killed the blood and fat were brought to her. The recipe unfortunately died with her, but they were without doubt, along with her potato cakes, the most delectable ever made. We would also bring home eggs to be put into a bucket of isinglass to preserve them. Taking the eggs out of the bucket involved groping about in the cold, revolting, gluey mess, and it was enough to put anyone off eggs for ever.

Dalley's grocers were next to the Food Office, then an

electrical and radio shop, followed by Charlie Stevens, the chemist, who made a miraculous chilblain stick, then the toy shop and Clark's cake shop at the end just before Martin's Bank. There were always queues at Clark's for their delicious confectionery and home-made bread which cost 4½d for a large loaf and required bread units (B.U.'s).

Behind this row of shops the police horses were stabled, the stables later becoming the garage of Mr. Warr, with the

Mr. Warr's garage

dancing class above. That then was the school side of the Village.

Directly opposite the school was a large house called The Elms, which later was bought by a Mrs. Vandervord who changed the name to The Priory and for a time became a private hotel. The house was surrounded by huge elm trees and a plethora of plants grew in the spacious gardens. For many years a parrot in a cage hung outside the door and was notorious for its wolf whistles which could on occasions be a cause of embarrassment. We all took delight in whistling to the bird and waiting for its penetrating reply.

Beyond The Priory and opposite the post office was a small shop belonging to Ashcroft's the painter and decorator which

Opposite the Post Office (now replaced by a row of shops)

later became Delahunty's. When Delahunty's extended their shop there was a tree which grew right across the entrance and which customers had to dodge round to enter the shop.

Crossing the road from the school was the Bon Bon sweet shop on the corner with Greenhalgh's fent shop along the side of Elbow Lane. Mr. Greenhalgh was often seen pedalling around Formby with his wares in a type of side car attached to his bicycle. The proprietor of the Bon Bon was Mr. Gilbert, a character reminiscent of Uriah Heep always wringing his hands and asking "Anything else?" Mr. Gilbert was never keen on giving change and always used his persuasive wiles in trying to coax his customers into spending every penny they had. Anyone foolish enough, or well-heeled enough, to tender a pound note for a penny box of matches would be asked "Anything else for the odd 19/11d?" Many of the young lads of the village would often go to the Bon Bon at night time after the shop had closed for cigarettes. They would rattle on the door, and down would come Mr. Gilbert who would never open the door, but neither would he refuse a sale. He would ask through the letter-box what they wanted and they would shout back their order. He always insisted on the money being dropped through the letter-box before parting with the cigarettes, and invariably he would push through an inferior brand—usually Black Cat, Robin, or Turf—and as he already had the money there was nothing anyone could do about it.

Charters' the butchers, Johnson's the cleaners, and Rawsthorne's upholsterers were next, followed by Elliott's with their open front to the shop and a blazing coal fire very often fighting a losing battle against the elements and being extremely cold and draughty where John and Janie Berry and May Holden served the fish, fruit and vegetables.

Duke Street: the Doctors' Surgery is on the left; further on the left was Sanderson's farm and slaughter house

Sanderson's, who owned the farm and slaughter-house in Duke Street near to the park, had the ice-cream parlour next door to Elliott's, and then came old Mrs. Smith's sweet shop. This shop was rather dingy and despite it probably being the most popular place in the Village for children we always had to be on our best behaviour. Mrs. Smith had a very brusque manner and would always put us in our place. Anyone entering her shop eating a biscuit would be told in no uncertain terms to go and buy their sweets from where they'd got their biscuit. In common with many old people at that time she had a deep mistrust of banks and was reputed to have money hidden away in the fabric of the walls of her shop. She certainly always seemed able to lay her hands on ready cash and on chocolate bars and sweets when there was a dearth everywhere else. Her shop later became modernized

Mrs. Smith's sweet shop, with Evans' cottage set back

with an attractive bow window when Mrs. Gerrard became the proprietress.

Evans little cottage stood alongside Mrs. Smith's and was set back with a long garden full of various types of flowers. Bennett's newsagents, with a gents' outfitters in one half of the shop run by Stanley Taylor, started the next run of shops where I queued for almost an hour one November the 5th to buy a ha'penny banger. On their outside wall was a huge blue and white thermometer advertising Stephen's ink.

Derbyshire's sweets and tobacconists were next, then Tilly Woodfin's cake shop with an ornate wedding cake always displayed beneath a large glass dome. MacSymon's the grocers came next and then Charlie Kershaw with his second-hand furniture shop. Charlie Kershaw used a hand-cart to transport his second-hand furniture and was a familiar sight around the roads of Formby. His was a thriving business making it possible for many families to furnish their homes, however sparsely, with the basic essentials of chairs, tables, and beds. Hire purchase was still a thing of the future and even when it was first introduced was viewed with great scepticism by many who had been brought up to buy only what they could afford. As many could barely afford to live Charlie Kershaw was a constant source of salvation. Another second-hand dealer was Mr. Winstanley who also flourished from other people's cast-offs.

MacSymon's (later Ruff's) was a very superior and high-class grocery store. The tantalising aroma of freshly-ground coffee greeted each customer, and the huge bacon-slicer set on the polished wooden counter was a fascination to watch in action. The staff of all our shops remained static with many starting and finishing their working lives with the same firm. This meant that regular customers knew the staffs very well indeed and received real personal service with the shop assistants almost knowing the customers' needs before asking for them. Harry Mawdsley, Joe Norris, Bill Norris, and Joan Rimmer (yet another one!) were just some of the long standing employees who remained with the firm until retirement, and no doubt their successors would have done so too had the firm and they survived.

The Chandler's, Formby Village

Next door was Norman's cake shop (later to become Ewing's and where my mother worked for the latter part of her working life until her retirement), followed by Williams Deacons Bank, with Hurst's chandlers and hardware next door. Then came Tommy Makin the barber, Alderson's butchers, and the famous Rimmer's on the corner.

Tommy Makin's barbers

Rimmer's windows were a delight to behold. Jimmy Rimmer, our local councillor who held office as the chairman of the council eleven times, was responsible for the fruit and vegetables, and the windows were his pride and joy. During the war years produce was scarce and the first banana I ever saw was when I was probably ten years of age and it was being eaten by a school friend, Ken Pinkstone, who carefully peeled and devoured it whilst we all stood staring in wonderment.

It was after the war that the windows of Rimmer's became the splendid displays they were. They were most beautifully arranged in perfectly balanced pyramids of apples, oranges, pears, potatoes, tomatoes, cauliflowers, onions, and every other fruit and vegetable imaginable. It was a positive art show, and the windows were never disturbed whilst the shop was open—all the produce for sale being taken from behind the displays. In the middle of the shop towards the back was the office with a colourful array of flowers and plants neatly arranged around it and where Miss Shan and Elsie Bridge carried out the work of invoicing and accounts. The fish and poultry department was on the opposite side to the fruit and vegetables with Bobby Rimmer, another of the family partners, in charge.

Once a week Bobby would travel to the family's other shop at Ormskirk with the lorry loaded up with boxes of fish and sacks of potatoes, and as very young children we would enjoy the thrill of travelling, along with his own children, on the back of the lorry, all of us rolling around as the old vehicle swung round the twisting roads through Altcar and Downholland on its journey to Ormskirk amid screams of delight from us all.

Rimmer's was an old established family business which like most businesses at that time provided a free delivery service to their customers. Every Wednesday, during the time my mother was employed there in the 1950's, it was her job to cycle around the entire Formby area to collect the lists of orders from their customers. She would set off for the Freshfield end and work her way back to the south of the village. This would take her the whole day, and in the winter months when the weather was often very bad with heavy snow falls she would carry out the work on foot. This would then take two days to get round, but it never occurred to her, or indeed would it have to anyone else, that she was doing anything unusual. The orders were then made up for the customers and delivered by an errand boy on a bicycle, or if too large by the van driven by Nellie Rimmer, another of the family partners.

Nellie was quite a character, very over-weight, and the butt of endless jokes from her brothers in the business. Whenever Nellie took her holidays her brother, Jim, would always inform the customers that she was off to Woodwards weigh-bridge to make sure the transport could carry her. He also insisted that she was paid a weekly wage by Raleigh for proving the strength of their cycles. On one occasion she was riding her bicycle towards the shop with a large box balanced

The famous Rimmer's (pre war)—now the T.S.B.

across the handle-bars. No doubt because of her size and the cumbersome load she was carrying she was finding difficulty in getting off the bicycle. She went round the round-about the first time shouting to Jim to help her with the box. The unfortunate woman was left to cycle round and round the island whilst Jim stood alongside shouting "Just one more time, Nell" to the amusement of all the passers by. After five circular tours he went to her rescue.

Throughout my mother's employment at Rimmer's I know what a happy shop it was. The work was hard, the hours were long, and the pay was low, but the general congeniality was quite superb, and no doubt very similar to that of all the other Village shops at that time.

One of Rimmer's regular customers was the very preco-cious young son of a respected local family. The staff were all mature women and dreaded the appearance of this child who treated them as positive serfs. One day he asked my mother for a cucumber which she selected and was about to place in his basket, when he sneered "Not that one—a decent sized one" and pointed to a large green marrow. Before my mother could speak Marcia Ashton leapt forward, snatched the cucumber from my mother and placed the great marrow in his basket. He paid for his goods and marched smugly out of the shop. The marrow was never returned, but he was decidedly subdued on his next visit to the shop.

Another regular shopper was Miss Ainsworth who drove around the village in her motorized wheelchair and would stop outside the shops and batter furiously with her walking stick on the plate glass windows for attention. How the windows survived her onslaught was nothing short of a miracle, and the sheer ferocity of her attacks never failed to have the desired effect of bringing the shop assistant racing outside to give her instant service.

All the shops closed every day for lunch between 1 p.m. and 2 p.m. One interesting incident occurred when Jimmy Rimmer had remained at the shop during the lunch hour and

The Village

whilst the shop was closed. He was busy in the back yard stacking orange and banana boxes when a young man appeared and asked whether there were any cafes in the area. "No" replied Jim "but there's Mrs. Trevitt's chip shop round the corner and if you're going you can get some for me". With that the young man disappeared returning a few minutes later with two parcels of chips and fish. They both sat on a banana box talking and eating, and eventually the young man rose to leave explaining that he was addressing a meeting of the Ladies Co-operative Guild which met above Alderson's butchers next door. When Jim later saw Mrs. Blackley, the secretary of the Guild, he (being a prominent Conservative councillor) joked with her that they must be desperate having "a young scruff like that as a speaker". "Mr. Rimmer", she haughtily replied, "that young man will one day be Prime Minister of this country". "If he's ever Prime Minister, then I'll be King of England" Jim retorted. Jimmy Rimmer was never King of England but Harold Wilson did become Prime Minister, and it was always with great pleasure that Jim remembered his encounter on the banana box.

Turning into Three Tuns Lane was still regarded as 'the Village' with Winstanley's second hand shop, then Miss Holden's haberdashery, Ackers the cobblers, and Soapy Smith's chandlery.

At the far end of Three Tuns Lane, beyond the Queens Cinema, the Conservative Club, and Mawdsley & Tyrer's decorators, was the second shop of Alderson's butchers, with Alice Mercer's sweet shop next door where she sold the most delicious home-made ice-cream—but only wafers—no cornets available! and where she also stocked anything allied to the Catholic Church.

Next door was the cake shop of Mrs. Parr. Mrs. Parr was a very small and bustling lady whose husband owned the garage next to the Police Station. Her shop was quite spacious but was completely bare, with totally empty shelves and counter adorned with paper doylies, and a huge mirror on the wall. The bake-house was behind the shop and a good fifty yards away and Mrs. Parr must have walked miles in the course of a day as every item asked for had to be brought from the bake-house. To add to all this trailing about she never waited, or asked, for a complete list of each customer's order but would take off at a gallop for a loaf, bring it back, then race back again for a cake,. and so it went on. All this quite unnecessary exercise must have been a contributory factor in her longevity as Mrs. Parr lived well into her 90's still making wedding and celebration cakes almost to the end.

Although these shops were not strictly considered to be part of the Village, they were all close enough to be very busy businesses. Chapel Lane (The Village) officially stopped at the round-about, but we still thought of the beginning of School Lane as part of the Village with Slater's grocers on the corner of Halsall Lane run by two bachelor brothers, Wilf and Neville. Theirs was a similar shop to MacSymon's, with a

Slater's grocers and the Library

long scrubbed white-wood counter and the traditional big bacon slicer, and the same aroma of coffee filling the air, and sacks full of produce on the floor. Annie Brooks was their main assistant until the business closed and she moved across to MacSymon's. One regular customer, renowned for her penny pinching ways, used to come in every Friday morning carrying a telegram form picked up from the Post Office on which her weekly order had been written—very much cheaper than writing her order on her own notepaper!

Next door was the Library in a tiny shop with Mrs. Derbyshire in charge of a very limited stock of books. She was a widow and had originally been a dressmaker before ruling us with a rod of iron in the Library inspecting our hands before allowing us anywhere near a book. Although the children's section consisted of only a few shelves of books the selection available was a treasure trove. Long before the advent of television the only home entertainment was the wireless with such wonderful programmes as Dick Barton Special Agent which we eagerly listened to every weekday at 6.45 p.m. always ending on a cliff-hanger. There was also Happidrome and Monday Night at Eight with some wonderful characters known as Ramsbottom, Enoch, and Me, and a slot in the programme called Penny on the Drum. We were entertained by the inimitable Tommy Handley and his ITMA show embracing such characters as Colonel Chinstrap, Fumf, Mrs. Mop and all the rest. Books and reading, therefore, were our main recreation, and free access to what could never otherwise have been available was a privilege greatly appreciated. Even the forbidding Mrs. Derbyshire didn't deter us from the literature which so enriched our leisure hours. Derbyshire's sweet shop also ran a small private library for which each borrower paid a lending fee. Quite a coincidence that two Derbyshire's should be concerned with our reading matter.

Next door to the Library was Needham's electrical shop where my grandparents took their accumulator to be charged for their wireless set. Living in Altcar, even as late as the 1950's, they did not enjoy the amenities of electricity or gas and relied solely on oil lamps for light, and coal for heating and cooking, and in fact when Altcar became electrified my grandparents were the last to be connected and resisted the change until the bitter end not wanting to be involved with such a new-fangled, dangerous, and utterly unnecessary invention.

As well as being a bustling commercial centre during the day the Village was also residential with many of the shop owners or their employees living above the shops, and therefore even at nights and week-ends when the shops were closed there was always plenty of activity.

This then was our Village, and these were the family businesses which served the community and which we passed every day coming and going to school. Not a super-market or building society in sight and only two estate agents, one run by Mr. Pickstone, and the other by Noel Evans, with Harry McNamee, tucked away on the corner of Elbow Lane.

On both sides of the Village grew huge horse chestnut trees giving the whole tree lined thoroughfare an air of grandeur, and the road surface itself was completely uncluttered by the total absence of today's hideous but necessary yellow lines.

In addition to all these Village shops Formby had numerous small general shops scattered throughout the area, many in close proximity to one another. Mrs. Mitton was one shopkeeper who had actually lived in Southport before emigrating to Australia in 1904. To travel 12,000 miles and take half a year to get there only to find a barren wasteland must have been soul destroying. To immediately turn round and come back again seems to add the comic touch. However, without that arduous and futile journey Formby would have been the poorer. Her shop was as dark as a dungeon and very small but was full of all manner of goods. The lane in which she lived was named after her but spelt differently. She lived her final years in a flat in Chindit Close and died at the grand old age of 104 in the early 1960's.

Apart from Mrs. Mitton, my grandfather's sister, Jessie, had a similar type of shop in Cummins Avenue. She had been employed at the Formby Golf Club for many years and late in life married the golf steward, Mr. Ferris, moving with him to the shop. She was a refined, gentle lady, and the complete antithesis of her brother, my grandfather. Like Mrs.

Devon Cottage, Cummins Avenue (next door to Mrs. Ferris' shop)

Mitton, and indeed the majority of these shopkeepers, she also lived to a great age remaining active almost to the very end of her 96th year.

Just across the road in Massams Lane was another general shop belonging to Hepworth's (previously Aldred's).

Mrs. Mercer was another old lady who had another such shop at Cross Green, and yet another was Butterworth's next door to the Royal Hotel. On the corner of Marina Road was Creek's general shop, and over the Eccles crossing railway line was Tickle's and Shadbolt's.

Nearer to our home on the corner of Church Road and Kenyons Lane was Rothwell's with Bob Hogg, Brenda Mawdsley, Tom Ward and Jimmy Seaford all serving behind the counter, not to mention Mr. Rothwell himself and his sister Elsie—quite a squash in a small shop, but large staffs were often essential for the personal service they provided.

Not too far round the corner in Watchyard Lane, opposite to Whitehouse Lane, was yet another shop owned by a Rimmer family. Close to our chip shop at the Freshfield end

Opposite the Police Station—Rothwell's Stores—Mayoral procession:
Councillors Jimmy Rimmer, Ernest Duke, Mr. John Breese, followed by
Southport's Mayor Alderman Townend (in the top hat)

of Church Road was Bradley's who also had their own bake-house and sold the most mouth-watering pies and iced buns. Bradley's also owned the nearby hairdresser's shop run by Nan Rimmer and ably assisted by the jovial May Hughes.

Only a few doors away Cranshaw's also had a small general shop, and yet another just across the road was Boardman & Tetlow's selling exactly the same type of goods as all the rest. Further again towards Freshfield was Mrs. Cairns on the corner of New Road, with Knight's opposite the Grapes, then Bell's in Southport Road. In Gores Lane was the very superior family grocery business of Dean's where they had at one time advertised "carriage trade".

It could be wondered how, in such a small community, so very many such similar businesses, not to mention all the independent small bakers and butchers, were able to survive and remain in business alongside the two Co-op shops and all the Village shops. The fact is that they did, and seemed to thrive, with almost all of them offering a free delivery service.

Returning to the area of the Village we had the Queens Cinema just along the road in Three Tuns Lane where we would queue up on a Saturday with our sixpence to see a cowboy or comedy film—usually Hopalong Cassidy, Old Mother Riley, George Formby or Frank Randle.

On the north side of Old Town Lane (later the Electricity Offices and now a block of flats)

In those pre-television days we had two cinemas in Formby with the films being changed twice a week and with two performances each evening and Saturday matinees, and at both there always seemed to be queues.

The Queens was the local flea pit and if the film didn't break down we didn't feel we'd had our money's worth. This was the invitation for all the chanting, stamping of feet, and shooting of bits of paper. It was the highlight of every performance and we were rarely disappointed. Sally Houghton and May Aindow, the usherettes, bustled about beaming their torches on the trouble-makers, and a man with a wooden leg hopped about doing I'm not sure what. If the fault in the film projection could be remedied we all then settled down to watch the film. If it couldn't we were all given free tickets for another performance—something we quite relished if the break-down came well on through the film. At the back downstairs were double seats (cuddle seats!) for the courting couples, and on reflection the whole building must have been very small but at the time seemed quite palatial. The upstairs balcony seats were more expensive at 1/3d than the 6d or 9d we paid downstairs, and always at the top of the stairs was a very large young woman seated on a stool collecting our tickets. She was the daughter of Mrs. Meadows and lived in one of the cottages just a few doors along from the Queens.

Amongst the regular patrons of the upstairs seats were a Capt. and Mrs. Hodge who lived in Duke Street. Capt. Hodge only had one leg and was presumably a casualty of the first world war. The films in those days were categorized as 'U' or 'A' (Universal or Adult). Even the adult films by today's standards were quite innocuous and children were admitted to these films if accompanied by an adult. For one first house performance a group of us had gone to the pictures unaware that the film had been changed and was an 'A' film. We were obviously disappointed and after much discussion decided to tag along beside Capt. and Mrs. Hodge in the ridiculous hope that Sally Houghton would believe us to be part of their family. The fact that she knew us all seemed not to enter our heads. We stuck close on the heels of our 'Auntie and Uncle' and confidently asked for our tickets. We must have looked particularly pathetic, innocent or enterprising because to our surprise these two respected elders agreed that we were with them and we all trooped in—to the upstairs seats when we had only paid for down-stairs.

Across the entrance of the cinema were big metal gates which concertina-ed together to either open or close the building. Down the passage way beside the next door Conservative Club all the bikes were piled, along with any prams or push-chairs which older children in charge of their younger siblings had dumped, as the 'pictures' was an easy way of keeping their charges amused and enjoying themselves at the same time.

On the wall nearest to the Village stood the large bill boards holding the posters advertising the films being shown and the forthcoming attractions. As a very special treat some of the cinema patrons would walk across to Mrs. Trevitt's chip shop a little further along Three Tuns Lane on the opposite side, but we always regarded her chips as very inferior to my grandmother's and never darkened the door! On the outside wall of Mrs. Trevitt's shop was a plaque advertising the Cycling Club which called on their excursions from Liverpool.

The Embassy, our other picture house, was quite something else. Originally a roller skating rink, it was bigger, much more plush, and sparkling clean. No necessity for the Flit spray in the Embassy! And it was a rare event, almost

Bubbles Dickinson's cottage, Church Road/Piercefield Road corner

unheard of, for the film to break down. The films, too, were of a superior quality both in content and condition. Glorious technicolour was shown as opposed to the black and white of the Queens. The box office was situated just inside the entrance to the left, where Stephanie Hilton, looking almost like the film stars we were paying to see, sold us our tickets, and the stairs ran up to the right. The toilets and washroom were at the top of the stairs in the centre, and the main entrance to the auditorium was directly opposite the staircase. This was regarded as the downstairs seats despite having had to climb the stairs to them. The back rows were always reserved for the courting couples, and it was probably in the protective darkness of the Embo where half the juvenile population first started smoking. A brass rail with a curtain suspended from it divided the front stalls from the rest which were always packed with youngsters. The seats were so close to the screen that it was a most uncomfortable position to be in, but as they were the cheapest seats in the house they were also the most popular.

In addition to the plebs, the higher echelons of our society frequented the Embassy, arriving by car and taxi—a very elitist form of transport in those days. Jack Mawdsley, the commissionaire, was always in attendance, resplendent in his gold braid trimmed uniform, touching his forelock with suitable humility and deference, and after receiving his tip silently cursing his benefactors to the ends of the earth. The moment the lights went out and the performance began Jack would beat a hasty retreat across to the Grapes only returning in time for the interval as though he'd never been away. During the day Jack was a bookie's runner in the days when gambling was illegal.

The queues were endless every night, and again the bicycle shed at the side of Ivy Cottage was crammed full and not a bicycle lock to be seen. Our two cinemas were poles apart, but one thing uniform to both was the respect shown at the end of every show for our King. With one accord everyone stood silently for the national anthem.

After the Embo the chip shop treat was at Ashcroft's—our shop—which was quite definitely supreme! The shop was situated in Moorhouse Buildings on Church Road and at one time had been the home of the Formby Council Offices until the building of the present Council Office in 1927 in Freshfield Road. Also in the same block behind and above our shop on the corner of Old Mill Lane was the British Legion

Headquarters where the Harden family lived. During the austerity of the war years when food rationing was in force the chip shop was a haven and provided the sustenance for many a family. The chips during the war cost just 1d a bag and the fish 2d or 3d depending on whether it was a

Church Road: Wilson's Garage on the right; Ashcroft's chip shop is far left

tailpiece or not. The cooking range was fired by coal and my mother, aunt, and grandmother—all very slim ladies—developed arm muscles like the village blacksmith with the heavy work they did; shovelling coal into the furnace, humping huge sacks full of potatoes, carrying heavy buckets of peeled potatoes, and heaving great steaming baskets full of chips from one frying compartment to another. As well as the usual chips and fish they sold 'fingers' which were chips coated in batter, and bags of 'crispies' which were the batter bits which had fallen from the fish in the cooking. All absolutely scrumptious but in today's health conscious society potentially lethal in cholestrol.

Tripe, cowheel, and pig's trotters were also very popular and these were delivered from James Mitty's, a wholesaler in Liverpool. A regular customer for tripe was Arthur Evison who ate it by the pound—never cooked and swimming in vinegar!

The fish was supplied by Ross's and usually came from Fred Sandys at the Freshfield shop opposite the Grapes Hotel. If ever there was a shortage then Mr. Price from their other shop at Cross Green would always come to the rescue.

Webbs of Southport supplied the crates of mineral water, and a wonderful character called Arthur Bulmer was the delivery man. He was one of the jolliest of men and after leaving our shop would deliver to the Gild Hall just across the road, and always had a lengthy session playing with Susan, the young grand-daughter of Mrs. Howard, the caretaker of the hall who lived on the premises. Arthur

The Gild Hall Band—Jack Cooper, Bernard Norris and Norman Brooks

married Susan almost every week, walking the length of the Gild Hall with Susan adorned in a net curtain and Arthur singing "the hen's last march to the midden".

Chips and fish were always wrapped in newspaper and customers were encouraged to bring their discarded papers to the shop and in return often received a free bag of chips. The shop itself had none of the refinements of today's fish and chip emporiums. It was very basic with a bench along the wall where the customers could sit down if there was a delay in serving, and quite a high counter which children often needed to stand on tip toe to see above it.

The airmen from Woodvale and soldiers from Harrington Barracks all poured in at nights, and many of these young men met their future wives in the romantic surroundings of the chippy. My aunt Edith was one, her future husband being a commando back from Dunkirk.

Our house had an ever open door for the families of these young service men, whose parents, worried about the attachments made by their sons to these unknown Formby girls, often came and stayed to ask my mother's and grandmother's opinion of their future daughters-in-law and meet their families. My grandmother, whose own sons were away fighting in the war, showed great kindness to many of these young service men and often provided meals for them at her home in Graburn Road. It was always astonishing how in war time with food rationing and severe shortages she could produce a positive feast. She had a store cupboard which was permanently locked, but on the odd occasion when we caught a glimpse of the open door were truly amazed at the supply of tins crammed in from floor to ceiling. She had obviously been hoarding the contents in preparation for just such a time of emergency and generously shared what she had with the boys from the camp. Years after the war had ended we found huge bags of pepper which would have been more than sufficient for the entire population of Formby. My brother and I loved these brave men who were winning the war for us and I am still in touch with some of their families today.

The King's Own Regiment and the Enniskillen Fusiliers were billetted here and their parades through the village were thrilling. The bands and marching men brought us children out in droves. We marched along with them in excitement, saluting when they did and clanging our heels together as they did. One young boy was so intent on copying our heroes he walked slap bang into a tree outside Mrs. Smith's sweet shop in the Village stunning himself almost unconscious. Out rushed Mrs. Smith, dusted him down, gave him a sweet, and though still dazed he was back on his feet and marching with the troops. The greatest thrill of all was watching the massive tanks rumbling along the roads and barely managing to manoeuvre the corners.

All this unaccustomed activity in Formby was exhilarating and 'the war' was almost just a phrase to us. We noticed, of course, that all our iron railings had disappeared including those which had surrounded the park and along the railway station bridge, as well as any householders' iron gates. These had been commandeered for the war effort, and posters were widely displayed warning us all that "Careless talk costs lives", "Walls have ears", and that we should "Dig for victory". Mr. Chad also peered down from behind his wall, caricatured by his long nose and fingers, and reminding us of the severe shortages by proclaiming from the hoardings "Wot no sugar", "Wot no coal", etc. Blackout regulations were in force throughout the war and there were, of course, no street lights. Not a chink of light had to be seen through a window curtain, and any offenders were heavily fined. As children we were never allowed out during the hours of darkness on our own. The blackout was exactly that, and was, even to the toughest of adults, a frightening experience. My mother came home from the chip shop very late one night and during an air raid. The short journey from the shop to our house on her bicycle left her petrified. She reached our house and with utter relief put the key in the door and nearly died of fright when a huge dog leapt out. The poor creature must have been as terrified as she was and had cowered inside the open front porch in an attempt to escape the howl of the sirens.

Motor cars were very few and far between, but what cars there were lay idle through lack of petrol (red petrol was sold on the black market!). Riding bicycles in the dark meant covering the lights with heavy material to dim them. Air raid wardens (the A.R.P.) patrolled the area making sure the blackout regulations were enforced and thus giving no hint to any enemy aircraft above. The A.R.P. were voluntary recruits from the community and included women of all ages from

The Auxiliary Fire Service (Jack Ackers is 2nd left)

teenagers to middle-aged, and those men not enlisted for war service which meant mainly older and retired men. Their headquarters were at Roselands and they also had an office behind the Food Office where they were under the supervision of George Squires and one of our local policemen, Fred Beswick.

The wail of the air raid sirens both terrified and excited us. Air raid shelters were allocated for different areas, but we usually hid under the stairs waiting for the plaintive moan of the all clear siren. Sometimes we could see the blackness of the night sky pierced by the beam of a searchlight. The Home Guard practised their manoeuvres in a field on the corner of Freshfield Road and Marsh Brows alongside the cottage of Mrs. Hale who kept goats.

Although Liverpool had suffered devastation during the May blitz of 1941 we were almost unaffected here in Formby. The odd bombs did fall. Incendiaries had set alight the pinewoods around the golf course no doubt convincing the enemy that Liverpool and its docks had been flattened by the inferno which followed. Carrs Crescent received a bomb, another fell in a field in Bull Cop, and four bombs dropped in an almost diagonal line—the first landed in the garden of

Clague's chemist in the Village where Tom Corless, the dispensing chemist, lived above the shop with his family. For weeks they had all been trying to uproot the remains of a massive tree stump from the garden without success. The blast from the bomb blew it out from the ground like a tooth extraction. The next bomb hit the chimney sweep Jimmy Meadow's cottage on the corner of Old Mill Lane and Gores Lane. Undeterred he and his family remained living in the house protected only by a tarpaulin sheet for the remainder of the war. Graburn Road got another bomb, and the final

The Freshfield Roundabout Garage which was bombed

one hit the area near the by-pass where the present Freshfield roundabout petrol station is situated. Shrapnel was everywhere and we roamed the fields collecting it all.

A plane came down in Duke Street park and I well remember climbing on it to see inside the cockpit. I slipped and fell tearing a nasty gash in my leg. Amid screams of pain I was carried to a house in Phillips Lane where iodine was poured over the wound. The initial screams were as nothing compared to the howls of agony as the iodine penetrated the wound.

The May blitz had left Liverpool in ruins. Whole streets had been blown apart and those families not killed were left homeless. The unrelentless onslaught night after night drove many eventually to leave their city for the tranquil safety of the countryside—only a comparatively short distance away but a whole world away from the nightmares of the raids. Formby gave shelter to many. Our home again had an open door, and I can recall coming downstairs one morning to find people sleeping all over the floors in our small semi-detached house. I had been carried half asleep that previous night into my brother's bed whilst my parents had given theirs and mine to these refugees from the blitz. Looking back it is difficult to remember just how many were in our house but it seemed like dozens. This was without doubt the turning point for Formby's village life. The exodus from Liverpool had begun. Many who had originally only sought a temporary reprieve from the horrors of the war found they liked the quiet country place they had found and decided to stay. Their friends and relatives visited them, also liked what they saw, and so it went on. Formby began to grow. And to change.

* * * *

Formby was a paradise of fields, ditches, trees, wild flowers, wild life, and of course the shore. There were vast open spaces and lots of country lanes for walking. We collected wild flowers which we pressed, and cabbage white butterflies which we pinned on cards and entered in the Flower Show.

The ditches were a constant source of pleasure to us and annoyance to our mothers when we always arrived home wringing wet. Time stood still when we were playing in the ditches, either fishing for tiddlers, sticklebacks, jack sharps, frogspawn, tadpoles, or even just messing about in the muddy water, reeds and marsh marigolds. Certain parts though, where the water appeared stagnant, were covered in a green slime which we avoided like the plague having been

Three different families but all Rimmers—Anne, Joan, Margaret, Derek, Billy, and Geraldine in the pram

warned of the dire fate awaiting us if we ventured anywhere near this natural phenomenon christened Jinny Greenteeth. We would immediately be swallowed up and lost forever.

The ditches played an important part in Formby's drainage system and ran all over the Formby area. Being very low lying there were parts of Formby permanently under water and when much of the building boom began in the 1960's many of the ditches were simply filled in and large areas of what had hitherto been swamp land became the estates of today. Some of these ditches were piped, but the old Formby people, watching the growth of the place, all commented on the fact that there would be problems with flooding in later years—a prophecy come true.

Most children usually stayed around their own areas to play, apart from during the school holidays when we could wander just anywhere, and as there were so many fields we had total freedom and safety.

Priesthouse Lane, where I was born and in fact still live, was formerly named Chapelhouse Lane. The name was changed in the 1930's because of its similarity with Chapel Lane. At that time there were only seven houses, all on the south side of the lane—two modern pairs of semis, the thatched cottage, the Priest House, and the farm. For so few houses there were an awful lot of children—fourteen of us in just four houses and ten of those named Rimmer! We were not related to any of our neighbours but we all called one another's parents auntie and uncle.

Apart from the Sutton family, whose children had grown up, we were the only Protestants down the lane, therefore all our friends attended the Roman Catholic school of Our Lady's. We all got on well together despite calling one another the Proddy dogs and the Catty dogs, and I got to know probably a little more than most non-Catholics about their church and religion (a subject never mentioned at home because of my mixed pedigree) which at that time was very different than in the present ecumenical times. Father Scott and Father Anderton were frequent visitors to their homes and just as I talked to my friends about my teachers so they talked to me about theirs. It seemed strange to me that nuns were teaching them, and they appeared to be equally as terrified of Mother Perpetua and Sister Theofane, otherwise known as Ma Pep and Sister Fierce Face, as we were of our Miss Reily.

Father Scott and Father Anderton

Fields were situated back and front of the lane which was lined with trees meeting in the middle to form an arborial tunnel which was very dark and spooky. When going to my cousins in Flaxfield Road I never ever walked, but ran like the wind through the trees afraid of the darkness even though the sun would be blazing above. A ditch ran the length of the lane opposite the houses and the unmade dirt-track road surface was a myriad of puddles on wet days.

Across the ditch was the field patterned with buttercups and daisies where the cows grazed. Blackberry bushes grew everywhere and we picked them by the tea-canful always using an old walking stick to hook around the bunches of fruit to protect us from the prickles of the brambles. Once the cows had gone back to the farm the field was our playground—jumping the ditches, climbing the trees, hiding in the brambles, making dens. And then once a year Wallis's Fair would arrive. Usually held in the Bay Horse field, but sometimes in our field, it was the pinnacle of our delight.

"Meet me in St. Louis, Louis, meet me at the fair". Every night the music blared forth. Formby was such a quiet sleepy place this cacophony of sound and bright lights was a wonderment of excitement to us all. The bobby horses were our favourite and how we were never seriously injured was nothing short of a miracle. Instead of sitting properly on the horses some of us would jam our outstretched legs on either

Bay Horse

side of the metal railings around the circular ride, and as the whole thing went faster and faster we would show off shamelessly, balanced precariously by just our feet and completely oblivious of how very dangerous it was.   Nobody ever chastised us and nobody to my knowledge ever got hurt. We wandered round the sideshows, eking out our few coppers and hoping by knocking down a pile of tins with a mop, or rolling a penny into a clear square we would win a longed for prize. We all envied the nomadic life of Valerie Wallis, the young daughter of the owners of the fair, and marvelled that any child should be able to live in a caravan and travel from place to place in such a different environment from our own.

The contrast of the Fair and the Bay Horse could not have been greater. The Fair was so vibrant and exciting. The pub so dilapidated and quiet. Lil Alcock and her sister, May, were the licensees of the Bay Horse which was so run down it was only frequented by those locals who were none too fussy regarding the salubrity of their surroundings. Until, that is, the arrival of the U.S. troops to Burtonwood and then to Hill House, Altcar. They must have viewed with astonishment this pokey little pub and they poured in. These were the first coloured people we children had ever seen and many of us genuinely thought they had dirty faces. Although we were much too young in those pre-sex education days to understand anything whatsoever about the facts of life we could not fail to notice the increase in female clientele once the G.I.'s arrived. It was all so exciting to have such activity around us and it was wonderful to ask these strange looking soldiers "Got any gum, chum?" and to always receive a packet of chewing gum. Everything, of course, was rationed and sweets were something we only got on rare occasions with our 'personal points' coupons.

Immediately next door to us was the old thatched cottage in which lived an old lady, Miss Rawcliffe. Originally from Preston, she had been a buyer at Broadbent's of Southport and was reputed to have been a real stickler in her job and rather eccentric, sometimes sitting behind the counter at Broadbent's with her feet in a bowl of water. My brother and

Priesthouse Lane Cottage in 1929

I plus all the other children from the lane played endless tricks on Miss Rawcliffe and would have been mortified had she ever caught us.

My mother's wash house was along our side path and against the privet hedge between our house and the cottage. It was a very cold and draughty tin construction housing an old gas boiler, a mangle, dolly tub, dolly pegs, and a washboard. There was no water laid on, and in any case the tap water was so very hard that my mother used rain water which she carried from the huge rain barrel at the back of the house making wash days sheer drudgery. An extension gas pipe ran across from the house to the top of the wash house on which my brother and I would swing back and forth totally unconcerned that we could have fractured the pipe with perilous results. The scrubbing of the clothes on the washboard, dabbing of the blue bag in the rinsing water, and mixing the starch were all normal routines of washday and all back-breaking tasks which in the winter were particularly onerous, and today in the age of the automatic washing machine and launderette almost beyond belief. My brother and I often climbed on top of the rickety roof and, hidden behind the tall hedge, would dip our paint brushes in jars of water which we then flicked over the top of the hedge when Miss Rawcliffe emerged causing her to think it was raining and to shuffle back indoors—a very stupid prank which gave us great childish satisfaction and something for which we would have suffered had our mother ever found out.

It was Miss Rawcliffe who named the cottage Stoneyhurst and who had the date shield placed on the cottage soon after she bought it in the 1930's. She did no research into its history but merely decided that 1613 sounded a suitable date and that was that! In fact she was probably about 100 years too early in her assessment of its age. She kept a pet cockerel in the cottage which went everywhere with her—even on the bus tucked inside her coat. In the end the bird turned on her and pecked her through the nose. As she grew older she became even more eccentric. Every Sunday lunchtime it had been my mother's custom to send either me or my brother round to her cottage with a roast dinner for her. This went on for a good number of years until she suddenly said she didn't want us to go round any more. She would still like the dinner, but it must be pushed inside the privet hedge outside the back door between our two houses and she would collect it from there. The following day the empty plate appeared back in the hedge.

Towards the end of her life the cottage became very neglected and dilapidated with the gardens so overgrown it was difficult to see the existence of a cottage at all. She died in 1958 and the next tenants were Mr. & Mrs. Jarvis who worked miracles in transforming what was a tumbledown ruin into a very picturesque home, but sadly a wattle and daub cottage of such an age fell to the ravages of time and in 1981 it was condemned. Although by now a listed building its condition was such that it was beyond saving and reluctantly it was demolished and replaced by a replica with the only original piece being the cruck.

We lived in close proximity to several farms, and quite near to the brook. The nearest farm was that of Teddy Mawdsley who lived in the Priest House which was next door but one away from the cottage. His pig sties were adjacent to the houses and the smell of the country was rife.

The Priest House was a very drab and unpretentious building erected in 1712 by the Squire, Richard Formby, as a home for the resident Roman Catholic priest. A plaque on the front of the house bore the inscription RFM 1712 which were the initials of Richard and Mary Formby who later became Protestants, and with the change in the established religion the house became redundant.

Many legends surround the house—of how Mass was held in secret there during the reign of William and Mary, and of the underground tunnel leading from the house to Watchyard Lane where a 'look-out' would watch the yard of the nearby church in School Lane to warn those worshipping in the house. The name Watchyard Lane was even said to be derived from this, but some of these stories have been questioned in more recent years and doubt has been cast on their authenticity. Nevertheless this is the stuff of legends and the stories have survived through the ages and could possibly have some substance. When the house later became a farm and was occupied by Teddy Mawdsley he stabled the horses which were used to tow the life-boat from its shelter in Birkey Lane to the shore.

We were fortunately on the main drain sewerage system and enjoyed the luxury of an indoor flush toilet, but the Priest House, in common with many houses, had no such amenity. Every week the marmalade cart (otherwise known as the lavender cart, the chariot or the plain and simple muck cart) would come to collect the effluent from the outside lavatory buckets. At first the filthy metal cart with buckled wheels was drawn by a flea-bitten old grey horse. As the buckets were tipped in the metal trap door clanged down and the smell was atrocious. Later it was drawn by a motorized wagon, but still its unsavoury load dripped along the route it took, the obnoxious stench clinging to the air as it trailed around the roads of Formby. A great number of households depended on the marmalade cart well into the 1950's.

Several different workmen had the misfortune to work on the cart. One was always in attendance. Nicknamed Hagan, his real name was Eddy Ruane. He had a bulbous purple nose, which obviously didn't function as efficiently as other people's or he could never have survived the years he did on the marmalade cart. He always sat on the back of the cart, and one story goes that Hagan's coat fell into the cart and he desperately grappled to retrieve it from the revolting contents of human waste. The other men yelled at him to leave it alone. "It's only a coat, Hagan, you can get another and it's ruined anyway". "It's not just the coat" he replied, "me baggin's in the pocket", (baggin being the local colloquialism for sandwiches).

The Priest House eventually came to an ignominious end in the mid-fifties after having been home to a large family of evacuees from Liverpool, the Hannaways and Morrises, throughout the second world war years. The house never enjoyed the facility of electricity, and almost every morning at a very early hour and in pitch darkness the young daughter from the house would be sent to either our house or another neighbour's for a penny change for the gas meter. Very often the only lighting was by candles which gave the house an even more eerie appearance as they flickered in the windows. Though very neglected and vandalized it was nevertheless a sturdy building of such solid construction that the bulldozers were unable to demolish it and explosives had to be used. A carved altar cupboard, presumably for keeping the sacred religious vessels used in the celebration of Mass, was found during the demolition and was removed to the Roman Catholic Church rectory where it still remains. The date plaque is now in the possession of the Formby Society having been retrieved by Mrs. Sutton from the next door farm. The house numbered 17 now stands on the site and one family of occupants were convinced they saw on many occasions, both inside and outside their home, a ghost wearing a large hat and a cloak and being in no way alarming or menacing. In fact they became very fond of the apparition!

The back of Chapel House Farm

Mrs. Sutton's farm was just next door, correctly named Chapel House Farm. This was very small and had been built in the 1700's. The farm consisted of just a few cows and poultry, but the gardens were always full of flowers, and on the occasions when we needed to take flowers to church, and especially on Mothering Sunday, all the local children made their way to Mrs. Sutton's and collected bunches of all varieties of flowers for which they paid just a few coppers. In the spring the wild daffodils were a picture.

Just at the end of the road, on the corner of Kenyons Lane and Watchyard Lane was yet another farm belonging to Ag Shaw (whose real name was actually Rimmer). Again this was very small but she kept a few cows and pigs and had an excellent orchard at the back. Her cows often strayed into our gardens from the opposite field wreaking havoc with our mothers' washing lines and scattering once clean washing all over the place.

Ag Shaw was quite a character, always wearing a long black dress. She had a large mole on her face sprouting

Ag Shaw by her farm gate in Kenyons Lane

the odd whiskers and would swear like a trooper when necessary. Five roads all met at her corner—Kenyons Lane, Watchyard Lane, Bull Cop, Flaxfield Road and Priesthouse Lane. On the corner of Priesthouse Lane was the old pinfold in which the cattle were rounded up. The pinfold had long since ceased to be used for its original purpose and was more a playground for the local youth of the area. It was constructed of large stones and divided into three compartments by wooden staves, with a door opening towards Kenyons Lane. The boys from Our Lady's School would often congregate to have a rare old fight inside the pinfold with all their pals looking on and roaring encouragement. When things began to get heated Ag Shaw would blow furiously into an old police whistle and the boys, believing it to be the strong arm of the law, would scatter like flies in all directions.

Along Kenyons Lane, and next door to Ag Shaw's farm, lived Humphrey Dickinson and his sister Marjorie, a very quaint couple who kept bantams. Everybody at that time seemed to have some kind of poultry. We had hens ourselves, and the foul smell of Karswood poultry spice, along with the boiled potato peelings, pervaded the house at feeding times.

The Water Board office was just along the lane where Jack Ackers lived with his sister in the adjoining house. Jack was a real character, a very happy man who walked with a slight limp, always sported a gold watch and chain across his chest, and had endless tales to tell. Whatever the disaster or emergency his only speed was almost stationary. A burst water main could be spurting water 16 feet high or someone's house could be knee deep in water, but Jack would still have to cogitate on the situation, consulting his book and licking the end of his pencil, before taking any action. He was a very familiar figure all around Formby with his Water Board rods strapped to the cross-bar of his bicycle, and whenever he tested the water hydrants and flushed the road he attracted hoards of children as a very inquisitive audience.

Across the road in the two old cottages lived Miss Petrie, who strode around the district always brandishing a walking stick, and next door Miss Formby, who had been a teacher at Our Lady's School and was more often referred to as Miss Annie.

That so many such truly remarkable characters should

reside in one very tiny lane was quite extraordinary, but Formby was indeed rich in characters, and not only our own locals but also tradespeople and others who visited the district. People like the onion man who came each summer from France wearing his beret and with strings of onions festooned around his bicycle and his neck. The pot man who called at the houses with a huge basket balanced on his head containing a variety of pots which he sold door to door. There was also the knife grinder whose treadle grinder sharpened our knives and scissors, and, of course, the rag and bone man whose horse and cart clopped along the roads collecting any old cast-offs for which he paid a few coppers or exchanged for a goldfish or a balloon. Our gardens benefited from these horse drawn carts, and there was never any shortage of manure which we would shovel up from the roads and use to fertilize our crops.

Turning into Bull Cop we passed acres of fields and reached Lowe's farm, or more correctly Devon Farm, the

Bull Cop opposite Lowe's Farm (now Gardner Road estate)

home of Jimmy Lowe, the asparagus king, although this was not the farm where the asparagus was grown. Lowe's farm was a paradise for us. Jimmy Lowe had four daughters all living alongside the farmhouse and his several grandchildren were our playmates. In fact, it seemed half Formby congregated down at Lowe's farm. Climbing over bales of hay in the big Dutch barn and hiding from one another was a pastime of which we never tired. 'Helping' in the shippon by strewing fresh straw, watching the hand milking of the cows and filling the milk churns, with a special treat for us to open our mouths and Bert Lawton, the milkman, would aim the warm milk directly from the teat into them. The delicious warm taste of the milk was sheer nectar. We brushed the horses and cleaned their harnesses, fed the cows and calves, and on reflection must have been perfect pests to the workmen, but we were never made unwelcome. We knew what was not allowed and would never have risked doing anything to jeopardise our chances of coming to the farm.

The milk round was our highlight. Early every Saturday morning at least half a dozen children would be badgering to get on the float for the milk deliveries. Dolly, the poor old horse, dragged round not only the milk churns and the milkman, but also the extra load of at least four or five children. The float was very small and we clung on, some on the back step, with the float almost touching the ground as it trundled along. Bert Lawton was very fair in deciding who went on board and gave us all deliveries to make. We knew our favourites where there would always be an apple or a penny, and if we were fortunate enough to deliver to Polly Ball in Flaxfield Road we got both! The milk round must have been the fastest passage of time in the whole week.

During the week two deliveries were made—one in the morning and one in the afternoon, but milk was not delivered on Sundays and the customers had to go to the farm to collect it. There were no such things as fridges and in the summer months keeping the milk fresh for just one day was a difficulty. It would therefore have been impossible to have ordered sufficient for two days to cover the weekend. Milk which came straight from the cow and was untreated in any way had a much lesser time of remaining fresh than today's milk which has gone through so many processes. It was our ritual therefore that early every Sunday morning my father, brother, dog and I would walk down to the farm carrying a huge enamel jug for the milk to be ladled into it. It never seemed a chore and was something we always looked forward to no matter what the weather.

When the October half-term holiday came round it was always known as the potato-picking holidays when a big majority of the Formby children went potato picking. I never went, but my brother never missed and most of our friends also took part. All the local farms employed as many children as possible, being very cheap labour, and there was no shortage of recruits. The Altcar farmers also welcomed the Formby children and some of the farmers sent a lorry down to pick up and transport the children to the farm though many pedalled off on their bicycles. One Altcar farmer would only employ girls as he considered them (quite correctly, of course!) to be more reliable and hard-working than the boys and they also did not spend half their time pelting one another with potatoes.

Bull Cop lead down to the brook, past the timber yard, where the boys would swim and where they made diving boards from old planks or tree branches. The trees were marvellous for climbing and very often a rope was attached to a high branch and we would all take turns in swinging back and forth.

The by-pass was very close to the brook and on Sunday mornings our friends who were lucky enough to have roller skates spent hour upon hour skating up and down the stretch of by-pass between Moss Side and Woodwards in complete safety with no sign of traffic. Our skating rink was York Road where there was never any appearance of traffic at any time and where we performed all manner of twirls, leaps and acrobatic manoeuvres.

All the seasons were a delight. The frogspawn in spring, the tiddlers in summer, the blackberries in autumn, and the ice in winter. The swamp was at the end of Bull Cop. Before the winter arrived we didn't bother too much about the swamp, but once the freezing temperatures came it was our playground. Up and down the ice we all skidded making long slides which sent us shooting off at frantic speeds, often completing the slide on our backsides. The water beneath was so shallow we could never have come to any harm had the ice broken and the worst fate would have been wet feet.

Every season of the year was an adventure when growing up in Formby, there was so much to explore and discover and so much to enjoy. The winters were much harsher than our present winters and there was no such luxury as central heating. Our homes were heated by open coal fires which were stacked so high the warmth penetrated the fabric of the building and kept our houses very cosy—the heat rising through the chimney to keep the upper rooms warm. Even the trauma of being ill in bed diminished with the comforting sight of a coal fire in the bedroom grate. Nevertheless in very frosty weather it was quite usual to awaken to feathery-ferned lace patterns of ice coating the inside of the window panes.

During the war everything was in short supply and at one time there was an acute shortage of coal and we supplemented our fuel with logs and coke. The coke was also rationed and my brother and I used to go on our bicycles to the Gas Works in Watchyard Lane for a sack of coke. We would then struggle home along with dozens of others pushing our unwieldy load to eke out the coal supply. We also collected coal and wood from the shore which had been washed in with the tide. Every single house had an open coal fire and disposing of the ashes every morning must have been something of a nuisance in many households. Down our road we had no such problem. The road was unmade and full of pot-holes and our ashes were simply tipped on the road.

All these coal fires necessitated the services of a chimney sweep and though many families undertook the task themselves the majority engaged the professional for the job, and in most cases this was the well known and popular Jimmy Meadows, a jolly round man who could probably have passed unrecognized without his soot covered exterior, his bike, and his brushes. The chimney sweep's visits were invariably very early in a morning, usually before 7 a.m., with the entire room being enveloped in sheets to protect the furniture from the film of soot which unavoidably seeped into the room, followed by the pleasure of being sent outside to ascertain the emergence of the brush from the chimney pot. A successor to Jimmy was Tommy Birchall, a comedian whose entertainment value surpassed even his chimney sweeping skills.

One year the winter was particularly severe and walking to our grandparents in Altcar was almost akin to travelling through the Alps. Huge banks of snow had been displaced on either side of the road by a snow plough creating what seemed almost a tunnel through which to walk. The weather was so bad that we were actually sent home from school one day because of the intense cold—the only occasion I can recall this ever happening throughout all my schooling. Instead of going home as we should have done a group of us went to Lowe's farm tramping through the deep snow and revelling in every footstep. I climbed a heavily snow laden tree and not surprisingly fell from quite a height into the frozen ditch below. As I lay whimpering in the ditch convinced that I was dying with a broken back I imagined the loving reception that would greet me if ever I survived, was discovered, and carried home to the warmth of our roaring fire. Nobody bothered or came to my rescue, and eventually I managed to scramble out of the ditch, by this time crying my eyes out from the shock and pain. Miserably, I limped home soaking wet, freezing cold, and aching in every bone, to be set upon by my irate mother for not coming straight home from school, for climbing trees, and for getting wet through. Mothers could, on occasions, be every bit as cruel as teachers.

We had three huge beech trees directly in front of our house. There were so many trees in the lane that the front rooms of our house were permanently in semi-darkness. My father decided that the three trees must go and he and his brother, Miles, tackled the job themselves. My mother was not only a little concerned that one wrong move and our house could have been demolished with the tremendous weight of the trees. However, their skills as woodmen were superb and each tree fell across the ditch and into the field in front, their length stretching almost to the blackberry bushes behind the back of the gardens of the Kenyons Lane houses. People came from everywhere to collect the firewood, and our fires were well stoked for ages.

With our roads being unmade they were like mud-baths during the winter. We were comparatively close to the main road so trudging through the mud for such a short distance wasn't too tiresome—we carefully picked our way hopping from one slightly less muddy patch to another until we reached the end, but our friends in Bull Cop were not so fortunate. They always set off from home wearing their wellingtons and carrying a pair of shoes. They would then call at Ag Shaw's farm and leave their wellies in her porch, change into their shoes, and continue on more properly shod for school or wherever. On the way home, they would again call at her farm to change back into the wellies before carrying on home.

The presence of so many small farms in Formby kept the blacksmith's forge in Liverpool Road very busy replacing the shoes of the horses of the village. Mr. Welch, the blacksmith, was only a small man but must have been as strong as an ox and it was a never ending wonder that the red hot horse-shoes could be placed on the hooves of the animals and nails driven in without causing them harm. Cyril Seddon was another farrier who travelled around the farms as well as working at the forge in Jimmy Dickinson's yard in Church Road.

Opposite the Liverpool Road smithy was Stott's cottage with a monkey puzzle tree in the front garden, and just further along was Pierces Farm, the home of Tom and Gladys Rimmer. This was where some of the Waterloo Cup greyhounds stayed when they came to Altcar for the hare coursing, and the familiar sight of the carriages coming and going from the Blundell Arms to the coursing brought an elegant air to our village every February. The coursing was an event looked forward to by many as a very popular sport, and sweepstakes were held in much the same way as for the Grand National. Public conscience has now reduced the

Stott's cottage, Liverpool Road

popularity of the sport which is regarded on the one hand as essential to the correct balance of the environment and on the other as an act of barbarism. Pierces Farm was not in my time a real working farm, the only livestock being poultry, but it was a most attractive place with well stocked gardens and a heavily laden vine in the greenhouse conservatory which was set along the front of the house.

Much nearer to our home was the small farm of Eph Walker, just around the corner in Church Road. His big Dutch barn was across the road in Altcar Road and when the threshing machine arrived it attracted droves of children to watch the work being done. Walker's were also very popular every Bonfire Night when they held a mammoth bonfire at their farm which, just like the threshing machine, attracted crowds of onlookers. Walker's delivered their produce by horse and cart around the village, and it was a terrible tragedy when their horse perished in a fire at Lowe's Farm whilst being stabled there.

Directly opposite our shop in Church Road was Bill Hunter's farm, on the corner of Cable Street, where he lived with his very large family of ten children. His dairy was at the side of the farm but his fields were some distance away

at Mittens Lane which meant his cows being herded along
the roads every morning and evening. Jossie Rimmer was
another farmer whose farm was on the corner of Whitehouse
Lane and Church Road, but also used the fields at Mittens
Lane. His cows often held up the Liverpool to Southport bus

The iron range, Whitehouse Farm (opposite the Police Station)

as they ambled along Church Road, and just like the horse
drawn carts which used our roads and deposited their
manure as they went so did the cows, making it a quite
normal sight for householders to come into the road and
shovel up this excellent fertilizer for their gardens.

There were countless other small farms in Formby including the three in Deansgate Lane of Dean's, Bond's and
Foster's, the farms of Tommy and Teddy Sutton, the pig

farms of Snowdon's, Baldwin's, and Brooks', as well as Sutton's, Mawdsley's, Houghton's, Aughton's and several others.

The second farm of Jimmy Lowe was called Pine Tree and was located behind the pine woods and sandhills and quite a distance from the sea. This was the farm which firmly placed Formby's name on the map with their luxury crops of asparagus being savoured by the aristocracy throughout the land. The season was very short, only lasting six weeks, therefore the work schedule was very intense. The asparagus

Jimmy Lowe, the asparagus king

was a very expensive delicacy and out of the reach of most local people, but those special favourites of the Lowe family always looked forward to the odd bunch of sprue (the thinner stalks) neatly tied in raffia as a very welcome gift. The asparagus was taken in hampers down to Freshfield Station to be transported all over the country, it was also sent by post from the Formby post office and again the counter staff very often received a bunch of this rare crop.

Not too far from Pine Tree Farm was Pine Tree Cafe. This had originally belonged to the Wright family, but had been taken over by Capt. Hutchinson just after the second world

Pine Tree Cafe bicycle park with Capt. Hutchinson's Rolls Royce and one of
the Nissen huts used as a holiday home

war, and like the Boat House at Formby, provided drinks and
refreshments for the day trippers to Freshfield shore. There
was no water laid on at the Cafe, and Capt. Hutchinson used
to bring down from his home in Montagu Road two huge
galvanized barrels full of water which had to be used for
everything from making tea to washing up. These barrels
were transported to the Cafe in the back of his Rolls Royce
complete with curtains at the windows. So much for today's
rigid hygiene rules and regulations! Pine Tree Cafe eventually
collapsed into the encroaching sea and today there is no sign
of either the Cafe or the Farm or even the sandhills such has
been the coastal erosion.

Being children during the war we were all aware of the
shortages and were therefore conditioned to expect little,

which must have been something of a relief to our parents who were in no position to have given us a great deal anyway. Despite this I cannot ever say we felt deprived, and when birthdays and Christmas came around we always received presents which delighted us although those same gifts compared with the sophisticated playthings of today would undoubtedly be greeted with derision by today's children.

My mother was the most marvellous manager of money, and on my father's meagre wages bought simple food which was amply supplemented by the produce of our garden, and made nutritious meals from practically nothing. The oven turned out delicious cakes and puddings for a fraction of the cost of those in the shops, and in our early years she made clothes for us by sewing and knitting. Our home had none of the trappings of today's considered necessities such as fitted carpets and the like, but the polished lino with comfortable rugs and mats laid upon it were the norm in most homes and perfectly adequate for our needs. To say I would like to return to those standards would be quite untrue, but to imply that we lived in abject poverty would be equally untrue. It was simply a way of life and we as children were content. No doubt our parents did have real money worries, but they lived within their means and were survivors.

We never went away for holidays and never had any desire to do so. Formby had all we could possibly want for recreation, and our day trips to Southport or occasionally New Brighton more than satisfied us. And, of course, we had the shore—never called the beach! The summers did seem to be very much warmer than our present ones and most of our school holidays, when we were not at the farm, were spent at the shore. The sandhills with the starr grass gave endless hours of pleasure, and with a pile of sandwiches we would be gone for the whole day. To save carrying a heavy bottle full of pop we always searched the shore for empty bottles to reclaim the money deposited on them from the Boat House shop, and then would buy our drinks with the money. During our childhood the Boat House was no longer used for the lifeboat but as a residence for the

Norris family—all deeply tanned from their fresh air existence. The Norrises ran the shop and cafe providing drinks
and snacks for the many locals and visitors who crowded the
shore. Going into the Boat House from the hot sunshine of
the shore was a sharp contrast, it being quite cold and dark
with a stone floor covered in the sand blown in from outside.

The shore was littered with wrecks and these we climbed
in and out of playing hide and seek both on the wrecks and
in the sandhills. All along the shore, during the war, look-out
shelters surrounded by barbed wire had been erected and
these remained years later creating yet more adventure play-
grounds for us all. The sea was much cleaner and this was
where I learned to swim and not at the Victoria Baths in
Southport where we were taken each week from school on
the train.

The huge enclosure outside the Boat House where we left
our bikes was literally crammed with hundreds of machines
and no thought of them being locked. It was incredible how
in such a jumble of bikes we never had any problems in
locating our own. The coastguard station was just behind the
Boat House set in the sandhills.

Dewberries, with their purplish bloom to the fruit, grew in
profusion all around the shore area, as well as around the
golf course, and we picked them by the load for pies and
puddings, going home with our hands and faces stained
purple from the luscious, juicy fruit.

On the way to the shore we travelled on our bikes, trikes,
or just our feet over the railway bridge and down Kirklake
Road. On the north side of the road were very few houses.
Just at the bottom of the bridge were the white cottages of
Gerry Walker with his scrap yard, and next door Kitty
Kavanagh and her sister Margaret. They were a quaint couple
and Margaret worked as a domestic help at the Roman
Catholic rectory. Their cottage, which they had moved to
from Phillips Lane, was set back from the road behind a field
covered in spring with wild daffodils.

Further along was Huddle Hall, and then the old cottage of
Joe Eccles, the postman, who was always fond of some liquid
refreshment on his postal rounds, but would never enter

Smallholding in Phillips Lane

licensed premises wearing his post office cap. It always seemed quite permissible once the cap was secreted inside his jacket.

The St. Luke's parish hall came next and then there was nothing else on that side of the road until we reached Kirklake Bank, the home of Miles Formby and his family. Opposite to Kirklake Bank had been fields of tulips grown from bulbs sent here from Holland, and then at the end was St. Luke's Church where the football fanatical vicar, Norman Cowden, officiated, always showing great reluctance to conducting wedding ceremonies on the Saturdays when Everton played at home

Going further south we passed one or two isolated houses, eventually reaching Stella Maris and Valley House. Stella Maris had been a home for destitute children before being requisitioned during the war for the airmen. Our school friends, Harold and Annette James, lived in Valley House— an enormous detached mansion almost on the shore itself. The birthday parties we attended for Harold were in January, and sliding down snow covered sandhills was almost, if not more so, as pleasurable as the time spent on them in the summer. The views from this sedate old house were superb with sweeping panoramas of the Welsh hills and the wildness of nature all around.

Not too far from here set in the sandhills was Tasker's old

c

shack. He was well known to all of Formby as the hermit having left his home in Liverpool to live the simple life of his choice with only his dogs, cats and sea birds for company. His first home in Formby had been an old caravan in the farm yard of Harry Snowdon at Moss Side, where he cleaned out the pigs, before moving in the mid 1930's to the shore where he built his hut from the odd bits of wood he collected from the flotsam of the shore. His only material possessions were his wireless, his books, his stove, and his oil lamp, and in this simple life he found the contentment which eludes so many. He always welcomed visitors, and only left his surroundings when it was necessary to replenish his frugal stock of food. He was never seen without his sack over his shoulder and his faithful dogs at his side. The local shopkeepers showed benevolent kindness to him enabling him to live his life the way he did, and he survived the elements for many years and died in 1965.

It has been illustrated that Formby was rich in characters, and none more so than Joan Holden who was a household name to everyone, although her correct name was Mrs. Dickinson. She owned two shops—one inherited from her aunt, Miss Holden in Three Tuns Lane, and the other previously Rothwell's outfitters on the corner of York Road and Three Tuns Lane, which became known as "The Junk Shop", "The Tatty Shop", or "The Harrods of Formby". During the war the end portion of this shop nearest York Road had been the Coal Office where Mr. Page was in charge of the coal rations.

Her York Road shop was a veritable Aladdin's cave and the most amazing place ever seen. The windows looked as though they were about to burst with the enormous load of materials and clothing which were piled against them. She and her staff always went to untold trouble to satisfy the needs of every customer, bringing down mountains of stock and never ever putting anything back. The shop ended up having a tiny walk-way through the middle with mountainous piles of everything along the sides, and despite always being in the most chaotic muddle the staff could always put their hands on whatever they wanted. Whenever buying material Eileen, Maisie, Josie, and Nora would always fling a few extra feet along the yardstick as "it was best to have good hems". The good hems often resulted in sufficient curtains for every window in the house. Joan Holden herself would have been horrified at such generosity.

There was nothing you could ask for and not be able to buy. If it wasn't there at that precise moment it would be obtained for the next day or so—and everything, but everything, was "on appro". In addition to the shop bursting at the seams with stock Joan's car was exactly the same, having barely room for her to squeeze herself into the driving seat, and her house and garage were likewise. There were commodities in her shop which had been there for donkey's years hidden beneath piles of pre-war articles never seen in any other establishment, and totally unfamiliar to many of the younger mothers who shopped there. Years after decimalization she was still charging the old currency with most items priced 19/11d, 29/11d or 39/11d.

She also owned property all over Formby and any empty and derelict-looking house would invariably belong to Joan and would most probably be housing even more of her stock. She was one of our real characters and probably one of the most popular. She was a shrewd business woman, deeply religious, who sought solace in her work to overcome the personal tragedy of losing a longed for baby and then her beloved husband. Her shop suffered several attacks by vandals, and shortly before her death in 1980 it was set on fire by lighted fish and chip paper being thrown through the letter box. She suffered a stroke following this experience from which she never recovered. She made a great success of her work becoming a wealthy woman and leaving behind her a legend and a huge gap in the lives of the Formby people.

* * * *

Formby was a very law abiding community with far more policemen than appeared necessary, all living in houses belonging to the Lancashire County Council and situated alongside the Police Station.

In the 1940's and 50's a policeman held a position of respect and high regard in the community, and although a lowly paid profession the integrity of its members was beyond question, and a 'bent copper' in those days was almost unheard of. Every man, woman, and child in Formby knew every policeman by name and they in turn knew all of us. We trusted them implicitly. Every night they could be seen trying all the shop doors in the village and then going on to those shops situated in other parts of the area. There were several occasions when my parents, coming home very late at night from their shop, had forgotten to lock up. Always the next morning they would find a note scribbled on the counter telling them not to forget again. The village, therefore, was shaken to its roots as was the local force itself by events from which some police officers never fully recovered.

Crime was almost non-existent in Formby until a series of burglaries mystified and worried the entire village. Formby was a very class-divided society during and immediately following the war. We had the working-class and we had the gentry. Most of the big houses, particularly in the Freshfield area, had servants of one kind or another, and it was mainly, but not only, these properties which were suffering the break-ins. As well as money and valuables even food was disappearing, and when a side of bacon disappeared from the modest home of Stan Lowe in Cable Street we all felt vulnerable. We were now at peace. The war had been won, and probably for the first time we were all afraid. Any residents leaving their homes for even just a few days informed the police, but still the burglaries continued. Then one night P.C. Brooks signed on for duty relieving his neighbouring constable. An hour later he received a telephone call. Intruders were suspected in Bell's grocery shop in Southport Road. Together with a fellow officer he raced round. In total darkness they saw the shop had been entered. They stealthily worked their way round until they were sure the culprits were cornered. They burst in throwing themselves on the two intruders who were clutching their nocturnal haul. The lights were switched on and the shocked face of P.C. Brooks was staring into the face of the man he had just relieved from duty. His partner in crime was an equally respected local shopkeeper. This may seem mundane and of little consequence today. In 1946 it was the biggest scandal anyone could recall. The policemen and their families were shattered. The public in a state of shock and disbelief. The offending policeman's family immediately left the district, and the remaining policemen's wives would not venture out so deeply were they shocked. The offenders were brought to court, found guilty, and imprisoned. The event was talked about for years and will probably never be forgotten by those who were around at the time. This totally isolated incident is not intended to embarrass or detract from the policeman's standing in our community, but rather to illustrate the changing society in which we now live.

* * * *

There were two real highlights in Formby's year—the Gala and the Flower Show.

The Gala: Queen Mary Mawdsley; Cushion bearer Christopher Rimmer; Dancer Pat Dockery

A Rose Queen seems to typify village life and Formby was no exception with the whole village turning out to participate in the traditional ceremony of the crowning and accompanying events. The Rose Queen procession heralded the start of the annual August Bank Holiday Gala with the lavishly decorated lorries from the local garages of Woodwards and Stevens & Hooks following the Formby Silver Band from the War Memorial to the King George V playing fields behind the Gild Hall. The crowning ceremony was usually performed by the Chairman of the council, and then the queen's entourage took part in dancing on the platform for the crowd's entertainment.

The fancy dress parade was always a delight and showed great ingenuity on the part of all the competitors and their

The Gala: judging the fancy dress. Left to right: Councillors Jack Dean, Bill Alderson, Mrs. & Councillor Jimmy Rimmer, and Pat Tickle

families. The sports and races followed with practically all the children of the village taking part in a wide variety of sporting and novelty races including egg and spoon, sack, potato, and three-legged races. There were always several heats in each race followed by the finals, then the parents and even grandparents participated in the adult races, again including novelty races such as thread the needle, slow bike, and ham cutting.

The highlight was the Formby Mile which was run round four laps of the outer circle of the field. This was a prestigious event taken very seriously by the athletic men of the village and the annual cup was a highly prized possession. The familiar names of Peter Bradshaw, Oscar Burgess, Harry Mawdsley, and Harry Jackson battling it out every year delighted the cheering and encouraging crowds. One year on a lighter note Joe Moss appeared resplendent in a pair of ladies corsets just to add to the jovial atmosphere and take the edge off the serious competition, but unsurprisingly failed to complete the course. There was one occasion when a miscalculation owing to the handicap of some of the competitors resulted in the cup being claimed by someone who had run one lap short. It took all the diplomacy of the parish priest to prevent an all out war erupting.

The Ladies race always proved popular with Nellie Rimmer regularly competing under the pseudonym of Little Nell— always running bare foot and with a very lengthy start, appearing to be almost at the finishing post before running a step, and always being overtaken by every other runner and finishing last each time. Little Mrs. Airey, built like a whippet and with the stamina of a horse, was another successful and regular competitor running alongside girls only a quarter her age. Almost every year in this race there was one particular lady who was notorious for causing trouble by claiming to have won despite the evidence of the stewards at the finishing tape. She could be relied upon to storm on to the platform as the prizes were being distributed and demand her rightful dues, making something of a mockery of the priest's customary speech about a good loser being more admirable than a good winner, as the complainant was being manhandled off the stage.

The variety of side shows had the crowds flocking and the Gala was a real money spinner for the Church of Our Lady of Compassion. It was a day of enjoyment for the whole village and the end of an era when it finally ceased to be held.

A step up from the Gala was the Flower Show which was THE event of Formby's year. It was awaited with great anticipation and was the place where everybody met and where past residents returned each year. Always held on the second Saturday in July it was for many years renowned for its good weather and excellent high standard. The farming classes were the main attraction with cattle, pigs, sheep, and horses competing for prizes, and all the local farmers decorating their animals, washing, brushing, and grooming them, with the manes of the shire and heavy horses beautifully plaited and beribboned and shining brasses adorning these majestic animals.

The horse jumping in the main arena with such famous names as Sir Harry Llewellyn and Foxhunter drew the crowds, and the Flower Show was quite rightly hailed as the finest one day show in the country. The surrounding exhibition marquees stood comparison with any anywhere, and the vegetable and flower tents were a picture, crowded with tastefully displayed exhibits from national as well as local firms. The childrens' tent was a particular favourite and reflected well the excellence of the village schools and the dedication of the teachers in encouraging such talent. Every school competed to out-class their neighbouring schools and the pendulum swung each year from one school to another in the number of prizes awarded to each. Classes were held in every conceivable subject from hand-writing and essays to pressed wild flowers and mounted cabbage white butterflies, from knitting, sewing and crochet to woodwork, art, and miniature gardens, from cake making to model making, and the judges had an unenviable task so high was the standard.

There were refreshment tents for the patrons and members, and also for the general public, a licenced bar, and a wealth of trade and country craft stands. It was a day when the whole village dressed up and stepped out to enjoy a memorable day in a carnival atmosphere being entertained by Morris dancers, a band, and many novelty attractions. Though the show has survived and in recent years been injected with new enthusiasm it is a mere shadow of its forerunners, and maybe indicative of our changing world.

The three Church of England schools of Holy Trinity, St. Peter's and St. Luke's had until 1938 educated the children of the village right up to school leaving age. In that year the High School was built as a secondary school to accommodate the older children. Originally called the Formby Senior Council School, then the Formby Modern School, and later the Formby County Secondary School, it was always known as the New School, and even today many of the older local residents refer to it as such. I attended the school for only a short time meeting children from the other local schools of St. Peter's and St. Luke's, many of whom remain my friends today.

Travelling up and down Long Lane to school we passed Rimmer's farm set in the fields and where an old carriage and a hearse were for many years parked alongside and in which the hens used to nest. We once saw a pig being slaughtered as we came home and the screams from that pig are as real today as all those years ago.

The atmosphere at the school was a happy one and the plays which the school produced were especially memorable. On one occasion Russell Brown, the music and art teacher, went with some of the senior boys after the evening's performance to my mother's shop with a large tin bath. She piled it high with chips which they took back to the school to feed the hungry performers. As the school attendance grew a prefabricated extension known as Shinto was added. The school had an excellent choir and competed successfully in several music festivals, including our own Formby Music Festival, travelling as far as Freckleton, with my contribution being as a member of the "Shrimp's Choir" and offering such renditions as "The Trout", "Oh, lovely peace" and "Nymphs and shepherds".

My main recollections of the school are of the cookery and needlework classes. These are indelibly printed upon my mind never to be erased. Both subjects were taught by Mrs. Armitstead, known to us all as Aggie Fo—Aggie I suppose as it was not too fashionable or complimentary, and Fo because when she counted out the numbers she always pronounced the number four as foe. To say we were terrified of her was an understatement. Miss Reily at Holy Trinity had been an authoritarian, respected and later revered. A more awesome presence could not have been imagined, and so, at the tender age of eleven, we went as lambs to the slaughter. Our first needlework lessons were to make a cap to be worn in the cookery class. I left the school after two years having un-picked the cap fourteen times, it still uncompleted and look-ing more like a floor cloth. It was quite commonplace for Aggie to shut one of us in a cupboard for some minor and probably unwitting misdemeanour. We scrubbed the tables, always scrubbing "the way of the grain" and waiting for the crash of the rolling pin on those same tables in recognition of some mistake or other on the part of one of us. Her temper was legend. In fairness, however, it has to be said that many of her pupils gained skills which stood them in good stead for life and have just cause to be grateful to her. I cannot in all honesty claim to be one of them.

It is only with hindsight that it is realised just what a difficult job our teachers must have had with such large classes of such mixed abilities, but whatever the standard of education success rarely comes to those who fail to seek it by their own determined efforts, and many past pupils have indeed attained success in all walks of life. The school ceased to be the County Secondary School when it became com-prehensive and took the new name of Formby High School. It was officially opened on 10th October 1972 by the then Secretary of State for Education, Mrs. Margaret Thatcher. That the school was such a happy place has been borne out in recent years through the popularity of the reunions, with past pupils flocking back to meet not only their fellow pupils but their teachers too.

From the age of thirteen I attended the Southport Technical College travelling there each day by train and always cycling to the station and leaving my bicycle at Alfie Formby's cycle shop close to Formby Railway Station. My brother and I both left our bikes at Alfie's shop as it cost 8d per week—a penny cheaper than at the Station cycle park. Both cycle parks were crammed full and it never ceased to amaze me how Alfie could always extricate the right bike from the tangle of machinery no matter what time we arrived back to collect it.

The railway station was for many years a joy to use. The porters, including Dave Bullen, Harry Bannister and Les Pooley, took great pride in caring for the platform gardens, and Formby regularly won the prize for the best kept gardens with a colourful display most of the year. The waiting rooms, too, were pleasant and inviting places with blazing fires in the winter and vases of flowers in the summer, and everything polished and clean with not a sign of graffiti or vandalism.

The back of Dick Goulbourne's cottage at the end of Duke Street (The Blundell Arms is to the right)

The porters often filled in their time between shifts playing bowls on the immaculate green of the Railway Hotel, and in fact bowling greens were an essential feature of every public house in Formby. There was great rivalry in the bowling league with many teams competing. The local hostelries of the Grapes, Blundell Arms, Railway, Freshfield, Royal, plus the Tin Tab in Timms Lane, Holy Trinity, Gild Hall, Duke Street Park, and the Conservative Club were all members of the league.

My father was a keen bowler playing at varying times with Holy Trinity, the Blundell Arms, and the Conservative Club, and reaching the final in the cup the year before he died to be narrowly beaten by Councillor Jimmy Rimmer. My uncle, Joe Ashcroft, actually died on the bowling green of the British Legion in the final of a match which apparently overtaxed his heart with the tension of the game— surely an almost perfect way to end one's life!

The greens were beautifully tended and created quite a pastoral scene when spectators were able to lazily watch the skills of the bowlers in the tranquil calm of a summer's evening. The age of the motor car has resulted in all these bowling greens bowing to modern day progress and becoming car parks, with just six remaining—the Park, Conservative Club, Holy Trinity, Tin Tab, Gild Hall and the British Legion.

The Park was really nothing more than an expanse of greenery, purchased by Dr. Sykes, our very respected G.P., and given to the local council to be used as a park for perpetuity—something, on his own admission, not entirely the magnanimous gesture it might at first seem as his house overlooked the area, and by this benevolence he was ensuring his home would continue to have a pleasant open aspect. A gesture nevertheless for which we all have cause to be grateful. The only amenities in our park were a bowling green and a putting green with the picturesque thatched pavilion adding a rustic touch to the surroundings.

Dr. Sykes was also a patron of our local football team which, following the second world war, was highly successful with a thriving supporters' club of which we as a family were members. We all regularly attended the Brows Lane ground, savouring the hot Oxo at half time, and followed the team on away matches to such faraway places as Burscough, Skelmersdale, Marine (at Crosby) and Prescot, travelling by coach and regarding the outings as very lengthy journeys.

Billy and Chummy Blanchard were stalwarts of the club and the cup winning team of the Moran brothers, Tommy Cain, Harry Gannon, Ginger Leatherbarrow and the like were our heroes. The football hooligan had not yet been born and

Formby F.C. Cup Winning Team 1947. Back row: Ginger Leatherbarrow, Arthur Briscoe, Bill Moran, Ned Moran, Billy Wright, Taffy Jones, Walter Paterson, Dick Sergeant. Front row: Dennis Jones, Kirby, Jimmy Ball, Harry Gannon, Tommy Cain, Taffy Edwards

the idea of invading the pitch would have been anathema to the supporters then. The football ground was also used for baseball matches with Hector Bonallo and his distinctive American accent a popular player.

Very few local people travelled to the larger clubs of Everton or Liverpool though many held allegiance to one or other of the clubs. We were not yet into the age of the motor car and the accessibility of the Formby team assured them of the local support. My father's visit to Wembley in 1950 to watch Liverpool lose to Arsenal was the highlight of his short life and the furthest distance he ever travelled.

* * * *

The church played an important part in my formative years, and from a very early age my father took my brother and me to Holy Trinity church with him every Sunday morning at 11

Canon Colin Towers Dawson

a.m. During our childhood Canon Dawson was our vicar, a bachelor who lived in the vicarage in Freshfield Road.

In our early years the congregation was summoned to the services by the ringing of the bell which was tolled by Ted Aindow who lived in one of the small thatched cottages in Gores Lane. When the bell became unsafe it was replaced by a gramophone record which was amplified from the belfry, but eventually it became very worn and the sound distorted and the bells were abandoned altogether.

The church had an attractive childrens' corner with a variety of books and appealing pictures and was where the flags and standards of the various guides, scouts and other groups were displayed.

Canon Dawson introduced the unique Christmas wreathing service in which we all took part. This involved carrying long garlands, made of evergreens by the women of the parish, which we paraded round the church. About eight children carried each wreath and the ends of each one were attached to a rope suspended from the high pillars near the roof of the church. We all walked up to the altar to collect our wreaths then positioned ourselves round the sides of the church waiting for the appropriate moment when Canon Dawson's voice would boom forth "Let the church be wreathed". The child at the head of each wreath would then pull the rope and the sheer delight as the wreaths all rose heavenwards shone in the eyes of us all. Sometimes the rope would stick or the wreath get caught on an ornate part of the

Holy Trinity Church

pillar and that would bring Miss Dean rushing down with her pole to release it. The beauty of the church at Christmas was breathtaking, and I doubt that any of our parents had a dry eye as the church was being wreathed. It is most pleasing that the custom has survived to the present day.

My brother and I were members of the Sunday School which met in the parish hall every Sunday afternoon whilst the Children's Service met in the church. I never quite knew the criterion for this segregation but I loved the Sunday School and the teachings of Miss Heaton, Miss Liverseed and Miss Walsh who practised such patience with us all. We were given enchanting little books with small squared sections on each page clearly marked with each Sunday's date and every week we received a picture stamp which we would stick over the appropriate square. I'm sure everyone else was as anxious as I was never to miss a week in order to get the stamp. Our Sunday School outings each summer were to the exotic reaches of Ainsdale Boating Lake or Churchtown's

Botanic Gardens where we eagerly explored these foreign parts and enjoyed every second. The church also had a thriving youth club where we played table tennis, snooker and billiards, and where we suffered, or in most cases enjoyed, our first grown-up dances. Across the front of the stage in the parish hall was a row of electric light sockets which never seemed to have any light bulbs fitted. We found that by sticking our fingers in the sockets an electric shock ran up our arms which caused us all great amusement but could have had dire consequences.

Holy Trinity church has always been used for the Remembrance Day services when all the local organizations in any way concerned with the patriotism of our land, such as the British Legion, W.V.S., scouts, guides, police and of course all the services from Harrington Barracks and Woodvale joined together on the nearest Sunday to 11th November for the parade to the War Memorial. For a good many years after the war these parades were most moving and heart-rending occasions, with the poignant last post of Jack Whiteside's cornet dying into total silence as "we all remembered them". The crowds thronging the Village were packed solid as the seemingly unending parade terminated at the War Memorial where countless wreaths or simple poppy crosses were laid, many by the wives and children made widowed and fatherless through the bitter conflict. The weather was always very dismal and often very wet and cold but the elements had no effect on the multitude who turned out to pay their respects.

When the war ended there was great jubilation throughout the land, and as in all areas of Britain we here in Formby held street parties to celebrate our victory. We joined with the Flaxfield Road residents to hold our party in their road. The long trestle tables ran down the centre of the dusty road, union jacks and bunting fluttering aloft, and despite the rationing everyone managed to provide a table fit for a victorious triumph over our enemies. We also had the privilege of the chairman of our council, Jimmy Rimmer, being in attendance, not in his official capacity, but as a resident of Priesthouse Lane.

Games were organized for the children, and a huge bonfire with an effigy of To-Jo, perpetrator of the Japanese atrocities, perched high on top was built on the field at the beginning of Flaxfield Road and Bull Cop where the sports were also held during the day followed later at night by the dancing. My uncle Miles was taking part in the men's race when he suddenly went into a tremendous sliding skid. His racing feet had hit a cow pat sending him sprawling along the field.

When darkness descended the bonfire was lit amid yells and whoops of delight and the dancing began to the accompaniment of an old wind-up gramophone and a piano which had been pushed into the field. For once we were allowed to stay up late that night and were able to remain at the celebrations in an atmosphere of great excitement for the children and sheer utter relief for the adults in the knowledge that the horrors of war were over and the hope of a peaceful new world was in prospect.

The Queen's Coronation celebrations 1953: Flaxfield Road street party

This community spirit was repeated a few years later when our King died, heralding a new Elizabethan age with the coronation in 1953 of his daughter, the very young Queen

Elizabeth II. We were still in the grip of the austere aftermath of the war years with rationing still in force, but with the Coronation celebrations came a wave of optimism for the future made even more joyful with the conquest of Everest by Hillary and Tenzing coinciding with this very momentous occasion.

During and immediately after the second world war Formby still remained the quiet rural place it had always been. Much building work had been carried out between the wars in the 1920's and 1930's when the Little Altcar area became built up with Altcar Lane, Marina Road and Kent Road providing what was then a very substantial area of housing with most of the properties being bought by the wealthier business families for rental to their employees and others. Small developments had also taken place in many other areas of Formby, but nevertheless the housing situation after the war was far from satisfactory and had meant that many families were living in less than ideal conditions in 'The Huts' in Broad Lane beyond the by-pass. The unhealthy environment and the acute need for better housing heralded the start of the council's building programme with the building of Alderson Crescent, Royal Crescent, Kings Close, Sealand Close, and parts of Lonsdale Road, Andrews Lane and Queens Road. Up to this time there was very limited council property in Formby.

I well remember one lunch time in 1946 or 1947 cutting through Long Lane via Alderson Crescent building site. I was with two friends on my way from school to my grandmother's house in Graburn Road. I always called at my mother's shop to collect my dinner and then went on to my grandmother's to eat it. The three of us were running through the newly planned-out site when I leapt across what I thought to be a solid patch of sand. It turned out to be a sand covered lime pit! I sank down to my waist, floundering about in the white sticky mess and getting further and deeper into trouble. I had raced ahead of my friends, Joan and Eileen, who stood looking on in horror as I thrashed about in the gooey lime. Joan threw me the belt from her school mac, and the two of them stretched across to yank me out. I eventually emerged caked in white slime splashing the revolting stuff all over them. We all traipsed along Church Road past Wilson's Garage to the astonished stares of the garage men and the fury of my mother when she saw my ruined clothes. The embarrassment of leaving a trail of white splodge with every step I took paled into insignificance alongside the reception which greeted me at the chip shop. I was sent to my grandmother's still caked in lime where I was cleaned up, whilst my mother had to pedal off home on her bicycle to Priesthouse Lane to try and find me something to wear. Children then did not have the extensive wardrobe of today's children and she had a very difficult job finding me alternative clothing. The indignity that day after all I had suffered in the lime pit was complete when I was forced to go back to school in the only other coat I possessed which was far too small for me and a hideous shade of brown.

Despite this council development the extent of the building

The cottage of Wright's Rose Growers in Halsall Lane (Safeways are now on the site)

had little impact on the way of life and character of Formby. The real changes were to come a decade or two later and were to change the face of Formby forever.

The thatched cottages were an accepted part of the scene in Formby whether they were the wattle and daub or the more sturdy and conventional brick, and up until the late 1950's over fifty were still in existence and dotted all over the area. The row of brick cottages in Halsall Lane where Bob Wright grew his famous roses were not thatched but were

The first pair of cottages in Halsall Lane (now replaced by an optician's and other shops)

most picturesque with a colourful display of flowers in their well cared for gardens, and the beauty of laburnum trees cascading their yellow flowers made a spring time show of splendour. The abundance of so many trees added to the general attractiveness and the tiny backwater of Furness Avenue was probably almost unknown to those not in the immediate vicinity. When the developers moved in to this lovely and rural corner and the cottages and trees disappeared to make way for a shopping complex it must have come as a tremendous blow to the Furness Avenue residents to have been so suddenly exposed to the outside world from their previous obscurity.

Many of the white cottages, charming as they were, could

Bob Howard's cottage, School Lane

not realistically have been expected to survive into the present age. Many must have been very damp and insanitary, and like everything else in this world had only a certain life expectancy. Unhappily some of the better maintained met the same fate as the rest when the power of big business stormed in and the few remaining cottages now stand as a reminder of our past and an enhancement to their surroundings lending some character to an otherwise mundane landscape of bricks and mortar.

Our village was governed by the Formby Urban District Council with certain aspects of local government, such as Education and Libraries, falling under the jurisdiction of the Lancashire County Council. All our local government officers were based at the Council Offices under the leadership of John Breese, the Clerk to the Council, and all of these officers lived locally, were known to us, and were easily approachable should the need arise.

The upkeep of our roads was largely the concern of the local council, but the main road through the district was the responsibility of the County and this was where Bob Sutton made his mark. Bob lived in Watchyard Lane and could be

Formby Council 1955: Councillors Ted Pearce, Jack Dean, Peggy Beeston, Bill Alderson, George Kershaw, Jimmy Rimmer, Christopher O'Neill, Mrs. Neep, Jack Hawkins. Behind: Harold Turner, John Breese, Ron Thorpe

seen every working day trundling his dust-cart and brushes along Church Road and sweeping the street clean with the deftness of an artisan. Dick Dickinson who lived in Altcar was the other Lancashire County road sweeper who looked after the Altcar stretches of roads keeping the grass verges neatly trimmed with the long sweeps of his scythe and often calling in on the residents for a cup of tea. Our own local council employees undertook the cleanliness of all other roads in Formby and many different men were engaged in this work including Tommy Tierney from New Road who tragically lost his foot in a road accident.

Our councillors were naturally all local men living in our midst, some of them the sons of previous councillors, and all of them deeply entrenched in local knowledge and history. In a village community life was comparatively uncomplicated, and expectations not unduly high. Our affairs seemed to be in capable hands and most people showed little concern for the matters of local government and were reasonably content. All this was to change with the enormous development of the 1960's when village life began to crumble.

As the influx of new residents progressed there was a desirability for these people to become a real part of the community and for some of them, quite rightly and properly, to become involved in local affairs. The inevitable result was that the newly elected councillors eventually outnumbered the older local ones. It appeared puzzling to many local people that having come to a rural area through its attraction as such, these same newcomers now found the need to change the image to that more closely resembling the places they had left. The simple life was disappearing, making way for the sophistication of suburbia with the accessibility of the big city. The administration of a small population of country folk by like-minded fellows with such local names as Rimmer, Dean, Norris, Alderson, etc. is now in the annals of history and though we still have local councillors resident in Formby their roots are newly laid, and we now rest under the umbrella of a much wider conurbation with local decisions being made by representatives not always wholly familiar with all the areas under their control.

In the fifty years since the war there have probably been more changes in Formby than at any time in its history. Today we have a population of over 30,000 and the status of a town. It is still a pleasant place to live and I shall never leave it. I count myself more than fortunate to have known Formby as a village—to have been born when I was, and where I was. My generation had very little in the way of material assets though compared with our parents were affluent. We experienced a war in comparative safety when we were too young to fully understand its significance and danger, yet old enough to remember it and even enjoy it. We lived in a less materialistic age, and though we had little we had wealth beyond measure in the freedom we had to go where we chose, when we chose. Living close to nature gave us an inner sense of compassion and love for animals and our environment. To hurt or vandalize living things be they creatures or plants would have been abhorrent. We grew up in a world of innocence and with a healthy respect for our fellow men. We were very, very lucky.

THE POEMS

Through bitter darkness and despair,
I sadly bore the pain,
Until the sadness sparked a light,
Which made me live again.

From all the wretched hopelessness,
Which seemed my fate in time,
The joy of precious days gone by
Poured out in words of rhyme.

Those simple melancholic poems,
Some happy and some sad,
Touched chords of pure nostalgia for
The times we'd all once had.

The copies flew around the world,
More tears than mine were shed
By kindred souls in foreign lands,
For youthful dreams now dead.

Not dead but just forgotten
In the mists of yesterday,
Brought back to life in times of loss,
To think about today.

The memories of a gentler age
Are treasures to be shared,
When we lived the simple village life,
And everybody cared.

THE VILLAGE

The name on the street map is shown 'Chapel Lane'
But that name's hardly known and not used,
'The Village' is how it has always been known,
And no one is very amused.

A traffic-free zone is what some people want,
Let the cars travel through others say,
Does it really much matter the locals retort,
It's been ruined and spoilt anyway.

The character's gone is the general lament
Of those old enough to recall
When the Village was just what its name would imply,
Full of shops for the needs of us all.

Old Bill Swift, Mr. Bills, Tilly Woodfin & Co.,
Just two banks and a shoe mender man,
Soapy Smith, Mrs. Clark, Charlie Stevens were there,
And they all fitted into the plan.

Then the banks and building societies came,
The estate agents, offices, too,
Accountants, solicitors all filled the space
Which big business had needed them to.

The family firms which had been here for years
Have all gradually faded away,
No Rimmers, no Aldersons, Elliotts or Wrights,
What a shame they weren't able to stay.

But the big chestnut trees are still spreading their leaves,
And the 'conkers' still blossom and fall,
And the children still come to collect them each year,
Though the damage they do would appal.

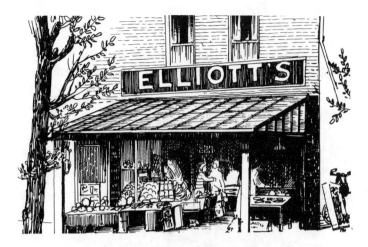

It isn't the same, and it isn't as nice,
But it's still not a bad sort of place,
Time couldn't stand still and we had to move on,
But we've used up so much of the space.

So 'The Village' is still what it always has been,
The hub of community life,
Let us leave it alone, let it rest for a while,
Just at peace from upheaval and strife.

THE QUEENS

A clapped out piano sets the scene,
With a woman sitting near the screen,
Pounding the keys for our delight,
Down at the Queens on Saturday night.

The noisy film reels clatter round,
Producing the pictures and the sound,
Not always synchronized quite right,
Down at the Queens on Saturday night.

No sleazy sex or violence,
Just films to cheer not cause offence,
Old Mother Riley or Pearl White,
Down at the Queens on Saturday night.

George Formby strumming on his uke,
Will Hay with cane and reading book,
Dorothy, Bob and Bing take flight,
Down at the Queens on Saturday night.

Sixpence, ninepence, one and three
Was what you paid for entrance fee,
Squeaky seats and flickering lights,
Down at the Queens on Saturday nights.

Sally Houghton and old May,
Flashing their torches down the way,
Ushering films in black and white,
Down at the Queens on Saturday night.

No one cared if the film broke down,
It didn't even bring a frown,
It was quite expected that it might,
Down at the Queens on Saturday night.

The slow decline in movie shows
Meant sad farewell, the Queens must close,
The lights were dimmed, we said goodnight
To the dear old Queens on Saturday night.

OUR LADY'S SCHOOL

I watched so sadly as a crowd
Of bricks and mortar tumbled down,
Oak beams and rafters sturdy still
Were smashed beneath the wrecker's drill.

This seat of learning once revered
By boys and girls of yesterdays
Had stood so proudly through the years
Of wars, depression, changing ways.

But now it lies a flattened mass,
Born of Victoria's craftsmen true,
Fine architecture built to last,
But gone forever from our view.

Praise God not mammon we were taught,
But somehow we forgot that prayer,
The riches gained from what we've lost
Have laid our souls and conscience bare.

Lost generations softly sigh
Beneath the tomb-stones standing by
What have they done that men may say
Our Lady's School has passed away.

VIKING VILLAGE

This Viking village now has gone
From dreamy lanes and spreading fields,
Where yeoman farmers tilled the soil,
And fishermen brought in their yield.

A far cry now from village life
Of blacksmith, squire and rural scene,
When cottages adorned the land
Their thatch from crops the reaper gleaned.

A simple, carefree, close-knit clan
When man would help, not hinder, man.
Where did it go? What have we lost?
Much richer now, but at what cost?

The fields, the ditches, lanes are gone
As progress madly marches on,
Where are the trees that stood so tall
And beautified each spring and fall?

The Rimmers, Mawdsleys, Aindows, Wrights,
Diminished sadly from the fold,
Are shadowed now by names quite strange
From places spread around the globe.

A sprawling, noisy, busy town
Which now transcends that lazy life,
Where residents don't settle down
But travel on to higher sights.

From both ends of the social scale,
Coarse diction through to cultured tone,
Few local accents still remain
As indication of their home.

To those whose ancestry goes back
Through countless generations here,
A certain sadness shows a lack
Of comprehension, thoughts unclear.

How did this transformation come?
Why was it here they chose to stay?
This village where life was hum-drum
Has gone forever, far away.

How glad are those whose roots lie deep
In humble, honest Viking earth,
For they still see with eyes that weep
The memory of their place of birth.

JOAN HOLDEN'S SHOP

Joan Holden's shop was a paradise mess,
Whatever you asked for she always said yes.
Buttons and tea-towels, slippers and socks,
Hankies, pyjamas, or shoes in a box.

Underwear, cotton reels, needles and thread,
Knitting wool, collar studs, sheets for the bed,
Trousers and dresses, ribbons and pins,
Tea-cosies, hair-nets, gloves for the twins.

Elastic, shoe laces, braces and bibs,
Dressing-gowns, jewellery, even pen nibs,
Material for deck chairs or curtains or skirts,
Buckles and hair combs, aprons and shirts.

Coat-hangers, belts, and hair clips and slides,
Cardigans, jumpers, and lots more besides.
In fact when you visited Joan Holden's shop
You knew you would never catch her on the hop.

Her passing has left a remarkable gap,
Where will Dad go for that natty flat cap?
Her shop wasn't classy, or tidy, or neat,
Quite the reverse, but it couldn't be beat.

Eccentric, hard-working, and totally good,
She'll long be remembered, if not understood.
With Maisie, and Nora, and Josie as well,
There was nothing you wanted that they didn't sell.

THE VILLAGE SCHOOL

At the end of the village was Trinity School,
Three class-rooms that's all, and three teachers to rule.
Miss Reily, Miss Culshaw, Miss Heaton were they,
Who taught us and helped us at work and at play.

Miss Culshaw was clever 'cause she drove a car,
Miss Heaton was pretty and younger by far,
Miss Reily, the headmistress, famed and renowned,
So tall and so frightening, she bellowed so loud.

She'd a voice like a man, and she had a strange hat
Which she wore all her life, we were certain of that.
At adding and take-aways and spelling too,
We daren't get it wrong, we were terrified to.

The fear inculcated by Lilian R,
Would be frowned on today as too ruthless by far,
But beneath all the bluster and outward veneer
She was kindly and caring and not too severe.

Now when we look back to the days of our youth,
We surely can say with absolute truth
We were happy though disciplined, safe yet prepared
For whatever life offered by teachers who cared.

D

BROWS LANE

The Village stops and then Brows Lane
Continues on with shops again,
Like one continuous thoroughfare,
But once those rows of shops weren't there.

The Post Office was all that stood
Beside the bank as right it should,
Then Trinity School was next in line,
Attractive building, stout and fine.

Right opposite a lovely house,
The Elms at first its name pronounced,
A change of ownership had meant
The Priory came and The Elms then went.

Great elm trees growing in the grounds,
Plants in profusion all around,
A pretty corner quite serene,
So normal to the Formby scene.

A parrot in his cage swung high
Outside the door, and passers-by
Would whistle loudly to the bird,
Whose strong reply was clearly heard.

Just memories now recall that scene,
Where such tranquillity had been,
The planners took it all away,
And nothing's left of yesterday.

ASHCROFT'S CHIPPY

The queue was a product that war time had bred,
It was something expected of all,
No shoving or pushing, no moaning or rushing,
We patiently waited our call.

Our rations were meagre, our money was scarce,
But we blithely accepted our lot,
With a war on we knew that things could get worse
And were thankful for what we had got.

Wherever we went to was always a chore,
But nobody seemed much to care,
The butchers, the bakers and candlestick makers
Had little to serve us with there.

But the busiest place and the much longest queue
Was the Chippy so cheap and so good,
It was friendly and warm and steam ran down the wall,
And good value was well understood.

The chips were just coppers and so were the fish,
And the batter bits tasted a treat,
They fell off the fish, cost a ha'penny a dish,
So who cared that we couldn't get meat.

What a haven it was, what a saviour of life,
It was packed to the doors every day,
Good hot nourishing food to feed many a brood,
And the mothers quite able to pay.

The soldiers and airmen poured in every night,
Met their girl friends and all of their mates,
They'd no money to spare but they loved to be there
In the best place to meet all their dates.

That Chippy was Ashcroft's—the one we loved best,
It was second to none without doubt,
They worked harder than most and sold cod that could boast
Would taste better than scampi or trout.

Those days are long gone and the war has been won,
And the Chippy well answered the call,
It fed us and reared us, it warmed us and cheered us
When we all had our backs to the wall.

Whoever would think that a Chippy could be
So important in war and in peace,
But whoever remembers that Chippy today
Knows the happiness served with the grease.

WALLIS'S FAIR

Flashing lights and blaring sound,
Bobby horses whirling round,
Great excitement for us all,
"A penny a ride" the man would call.

Round and round the horses flew,
Children screaming as they do
When wild excitement reaches heights,
Amid the maze of fairy lights.

The whole of Formby came each night
To sample all the fair's delights,
The Bay Horse field was quite transformed,
And everybody's hearts were warmed.

They'd all the things to bring real joy
To man and woman, girl and boy,
Rolling pennies, throwing mops,
Swingboats, waltzers—they were tops.

You'd even win a threepenny bit
If all the tins your mop could hit,
And then you'd have another go
To try again with one more throw.

Too soon the week would fly away,
The caravans packed and on their way,
The lights extinguished, music gone,
Wallis's Fair was travelling on.

THE SHORE

Long summer days,
School holidays,
Always it seemed to be warm,
Sandwiches packed,
Off we all tracked
To the shore like bees in a swarm.

Off on our bikes,
Even on trikes,
Our parents knew we were fine,
Sun, sand and sea,
Nothing could be
Better for kids at that time.

Sandhills were steep,
Starr grass grew deep,
We ran and chased through it all,
Laughter and joy
For each girl and boy,
Tossing an old tennis ball.

Nothing to pay,
Free every day,
We splashed and swam in the waves,
Jellyfish found,
Digging around,
Sand tunnels made into caves.

Exotic shells,
Lovely harebells,
Pebbles so smooth and so round,
Morning till night,
Loving the sight
Of the sea washing in on the ground.

Tired and spent,
Dirty we went
Back home exhausted to bed,
Happy to be
Here in Formby,
With our playground the shore just ahead.

RIMMER'S

On the corner of the village was a shop,
With the name emblazoned right across the top,
That name was part of Formby's heritage,
Quite symbolic of our former Viking age.

Rimmer's was that proud and famous name,
And their shop was full of fruit and fish and game,
Their windows were a lovely sight to see,
Piled with fruit and veg. in perfect symmetry.

Great huge pyramids of apples firm and round,
Next to oranges shaped in a perfect mound,
All the veg's you could ever hope to need,
Neatly stacked and on display for us to feed.

Mr. Jim was on the side with all the fruit,
And Mr. Bob the fish and poultry followed suit,
Mr. Bill the market transport organized,
And Miss Nellie ran the van delivery side.

Miss Shan and Elsie Bridge kept the accounts,
While Dixie Ashton weighed the fish in right amounts,
Mrs. Rimmer, Mrs. Ward and Marcia, too,
Along with Betha made a really first-class crew.

For a hundred years the family served us well,
And they always would as far as we could tell,
But there sadly dawned the day the blinds came down,
When our village woke and found it was a town.

THE PRIEST HOUSE

The Roman Catholic faith was strong,
And tolerated in that day,
A church was needed for the throng
Of worshippers to kneel and pray.

The church was built along School Lane,
And mass was celebrated there,
Until the Orange monarchs came
And put an end to sacred prayer.

The Priest house standing quite close by,
So stoutly built by Formby's squire,
Stood empty now and wondered why
God's love for man by man should tire.

Religious differences prevailed,
And Catholics once more were outcast,
Their hearts were rent, they wept and wailed,
But still their faith held strong and fast.

Their church for worship was closed down,
But that would not deter the flock,
The Lord with mercies would them crown,
Their faith would stand firm as a rock.

Chapelhouse Farm

In secret they assembled then,
Along the lane at the Priest house,
"Watch yard" the cry would warn the men
To hide and keep quiet as a mouse.

Two hundred years have rolled away,
The fortunes of the house have changed,
Irreverence followed till the day
Its use was fully rearranged.

A farm house later it became,
With pigs and cows around the land,
Old Teddy Mawdsley was the name
Of the new occupant on hand.

The Priest house days were numbered now,
Another war had sealed its fate,
Evacuees replaced the cows,
Soon history would evaporate.

The 1950's came around,
And Formby's building boom began,
That great historic house came down,
A victim of expansion's plan.

Those unconcerned with history
See just a pleasant road today,
Religious strife and mystery
Lost in the past of yesterday.

THE MAY BLITZ

A direct hit from Jerry's bomb
Made Liverpool look like the Somme.
Where can we go? What shall we do?
Our homes are gone, our families too.

A dreadful week with no respite
From Hitler's wrath and Nazi might,
The terrace houses all aflame,
What price to pay in freedom's name.

Why is this happening to our port?
The people's war is being fought.
Why pick on us? What have we done
To tantalize and rile the Hun?

A full week passed and still they came,
The messerschmits to kill and maim,
The awful carnage, blazing fires,
The sky alight like funeral pyres.

We've had enough, we'll have to go,
Our friends in Formby, they will know
Where we can rest and get away
From all this horror night and day.

So weary—just for peace they pined,
By any means that they could find
They left their ruined city for
Some refuge from that evil war.

What utter bliss, what calm and peace,
True friends to help, the noise to cease,
Refreshed, restored in clean fresh air,
A world away from fear and care.

The Blitz was done, the city scarred,
What bits were left were black and charred,
But Churchill said we'd win the war,
We knew we could—we'd win, and more.

The city would be built again,
Lots of the people would remain,
But Formby's rural country face
Would see a change affect the place.

And so it was—it grew and grew,
And lost the charm the locals knew.
The war must take most of the blame
Why Formby now is not the same.

FORMBY

We knew it once when we were small,
But did we really see at all
The beauty we just took as ours,
Whilst playing in the fields for hours.

The trees we climbed and hid inside,
Their trunks and branches spreading wide,
The brambles scratching racing legs,
The birds' nests full of speckled eggs.

The farmyard barns with bales of hay,
Beside the shippon where each day
The milkman's hands coaxed forth the milk
With rhythmic movement smooth as silk.

The countryside which met the sea,
Wide open spaces, wild and free,
The seagulls wheeling overhead,
How will it look when we are dead?

No fields, no farms, no trees to climb,
Our children now don't have the time,
Life rushed away at frantic pace,
We hurtled on through time and space.

We were to blame, we did not try,
Whilst living we let Formby die,
It grew, it flourished, then it burst,
We watched as progress did its worst.

Our ghostly spectres now look down
On an affluent suburban town,
And shake each sad bewildered head,
At how it looks now we are dead.

CHURCH ROAD

From the top of Church Road right down to Cross Green,
What a mixture of rural delight,
Some nice houses, three farms, several shops and a school,
With the police station there on the right.

Bubbles Dickinson's hardware and chandlery shop,
Right opposite Greenhalgh's place,
Mrs. Cairns on the corner past Bobby Neale's pies,
And the cafe for feeding your face.

Bradley's, Yeoman's, then Cranshaw's, and Tommy McGee
Cutting hair for a tanner a go,
Mr. Golding and 'Brookie' with mouths full of tacks,
Mending shoes with a new heel or toe.

Ashcroft's chip shop came next, and then over the road
Frankie Wright with a marvellous stock
Of cigarettes, sweets and a host of good things
From a tea pot to carbolic block.

Next door Boardman & Tetlow's for grocery goods,
And the Co-op just opposite there,
Wilson's garage for petrol for automobiles,
And a pump to fill tyres full of air.

The Gild Hall so popular Saturday nights,
Where the girls met their future husband
At the dances with Bernard and Norman and Jack,
Playing well in their fine three piece band.

Police Station and Whitehouse Farm

Bill Hunter's farm first, Jossie Rimmer's the next,
And their cows used the road like a track,
Herding along from the farms to the fields,
Then for milking they all herded back.

The rosy red apples on Jossie's big trees
Were temptation to all of the boys,
But six policemen right opposite worked like a charm
And the orchard was safe from their ploys.

Next to the police station old Mr. Parr,
With his garage constructed of tin,
He mended our punctures and fixed up our bikes,
And sold cans full of blue paraffin.

Rothwell's stores were across with Bob Hogg at the till,
Serving bacon and bread and the like,
Very handy for mothers who met out their tots
From Our Lady's at four every night.

Stevens & Hooks with their haulage firm next,
Past the school where Ma Pep ruled the roost,
Then the Bay Horse with Alcocks, both Lily and May,
So run down they'd no business to boost.

Some more great big houses, then right at the end
Walker's Farm with the pony to stroke,
What a wonderful stroll down a major main road,
Where each step of the way someone spoke.

For those who recall those far halcyon days,
When our lives were much simpler than now,
We were lucky to know just what Formby was like
When the village lived under the plough.

TO THE BROOK

Straight down Bull Cop and out over the field,
Hop over the stile, our happiness sealed,
With jam jars and fishing nets and old tin cans
Clutched tightly for what we could catch with our hands.

Our fishing nets made with a nail and a cane,
Old stockings the net as we ran down the lane
To the ditch by the brook where the tiddlers and frogs
And jack sharps swam round in the reeds and the logs.

All day we would play catching all that we could,
Fill the jam jars with tiddlers and handfuls of mud,
Then back home we went past the barn and Lowe's Farm,
Scruffy children wet through but free from all harm.

What a great way of life with no worries or cares,
A tin bath in the living room, then up the stairs
To our dreams of tomorrow when we'd all start again
With our jam jars and fishing nets off down the lane.

THE GALA

Bank Holiday Monday, the sun always shone,
The village turned out, every single last one,
To join in the races and happy side shows,
And meet all the neighbours that everyone knows.

The rose queen so pretty with full retinue,
The band playing well as they came into view,
Along to the field just behind the Gild Hall,
Where the longed for performance was waiting for all.

PROGRAMME.

Children's Fancy Dress Parade.

Parade at War Memorial at 1-30 p.m. prompt.
Interval 5 to 5-45 p.m.
Refreshments at Moderate Prices in the Hall.

The Committee has power to alter any handicap.

EVENT 1—*100 Yards Flat Race, Men.*

	HEAT 1			yds		HEAT 2			
1	H. Lamar	...	...	4	9	Jas. Lloyd	...	...	1
2	W. Rimmer, C.L.	...	...	7	10	H. Cockcroft	...	...	4
3	Hy. Jackson	...	...	7	11	John Fenner	...	...	7
4	Ed. Mawdsley	...	...	8	12	Ted Edwards	...	...	8
5	R. G. Norris	...	...	10	13	W. H. Hall	...	...	10
6	R. Leddy	...	...	13	14	John Barton	...	...	13
7	E. Moon	...	...	13	15	R. Wareing	...	...	4
8	Jas. Rimmer, C.L.	...	...	8					
	1st	2nd				1st		2nd	

HEAT 3

16	D. Postlethwaite	...	...	5
17	S. Scarisbrick	...	...	7
18	Jos. Mawdsley, M'H.	...	...	7
19	Jos. Rimmer, L.A.	...	...	9
20	Jos. Steneth	...	...	9
21	Hy. Mawdsley	...	...	13
22	D. Salmon	...	...	1
23	J. Moore	...	...	4
	1st		2nd	

Descend from the wagons then on to the stage,
Where the rose queen sat down helped along by her page,
The crowning was done and we all clapped and cheered,
The photographer snapped them and then disappeared.

The kid's fancy dress was a popular class,
With Snow White, Formby's triplets, a big beer glass,
Such ingenious ideas made from old odds and ends,
By the Mums and the Dads and the aunties and friends.

E

The sports and the races of all different kinds,
The children excited and out of their minds
At the prospect of winning a prize or a cup
If they got to the finish without tripping up.

The sack race, obstacles, plain running track,
The ladies race with 'Little Nell' at the back,
She was such a good sport, overweight and rotund,
But she ran like a good 'un to swell the church fund.

The highlight was always the great Formby Mile,
As the men and the boys set off with a smile,
Peter Bradshaw, the champion, was there at the last,
To pick up the cup as the winning post passed.

Tommy Ledger was shouting and taking the cash,
As the big 'Wheel of Fortune' whizzed round in a flash,
When the finger stopped moving and came home to rest,
You knew if you'd lost or had feathered your nest.

That August Bank Holiday came every year,
Accepted and cherished as something held dear,
But as our sleepy village grew up and got lost,
A whole way of life disappeared to our cost.

Wicks Lane, near
Green Loons Farm

BYGONE DAYS

Country folk with country accents,
Everyone knew everyone,
Leafy lanes and grassy meadows,
No one thought of rushing on.

Buttercups and four leaf clover,
Celandine and hollyhocks,
Flowers growing in the hedgerows,
Children blowing dandelion clocks.

Lots of dusty lanes to wander,
Daisy chains and marigolds,
Many ditches filled with frogspawn,
Cattle in the old pinfolds.

Making hay from dawn till sunset,
Stooks of corn set in the fields,
Farmers bringing in the harvest,
Toiling as the church bell peals.

Butterflies fluttering gently round us,
Autumn conkers on a string,
Oak and elm and ash and poplar,
Sycamore pods fly like a wing.

Blackberry picking in the evenings,
Dewberries growing by the shore,
Gorse and vetch and foxgloves blooming,
Who could ever ask for more?

Is this memory just a daydream,
Passed and gone just like a kiss?
How can we convince our children
Formby once was just like this?

TASKER

A tumble-down shack and a man from the wars,
Whose life seemed so simple without any cause,
Some old mongrel dogs and a battered tin pan,
The sandhills were home to this solitary man.

We knew him as Tasker and thought him quite odd,
A remote and strange character, off he would plod
With down-at-heel shoes and tattered old togs,
As he trailed from the shore with his sack and his dogs.

His knowledge and culture belied by his looks,
His life just revolved round his pets and his books,
He'd rejected a world he could not comprehend
For the plants and the wild life that nature would send.

He lived very frugally, liked his pint pot,
The cold and the wet seemed to bother him not,
Throughout all the seasons his life was the same,
He survived snow and rain and when the winds came.

Looked down on by many for what he commends,
His dogs were his family, the seagulls his friends,
His life style for him was contentment sublime,
And to live close to nature was never a crime.

No home, no possessions, no job, and no wife,
He did nothing, went nowhere, wasted his life,
Why should we remember and talk of him still?
He's part of our folk-lore, and that's why we will.

THE EMBASSY

The Embassy cinema so plush and so grand,
Where the lads and the lasses would go hand in hand,
Jack Mawdsley in uniform smartly attired,
Greeting the patrons, both young and retired.

A clip round the ear if the boys misbehaved,
Then across to the Grapes for his thirst to be saved,
Back for the interval shining his light,
As though he'd been there for the whole of the night.

Stephanie Hilton was there at the box office flap,
Our tickets shot out from a brass ticket trap,
We'd then go inside as the queue moved along,
Take our seats for the show which would never go wrong.

Red velvet seats, well upholstered and clean,
Lovely carpets, posh lights and a big flashy screen,
This was no flea pit for any old scruffs,
The elite were the patrons in fur coats and muffs.

Two-and-threes up the stairs to the balcony seats,
Where the upper crust classes would go for their treats,
Technicolour films with no hitches or gaffes,
And cartoons designed to produce lots of laughs.

Downstairs in the one-and-nines on the back row
Were the sweethearts who always missed half of the show,
Paying far more attention to what went on there,
Than to watching the dancing of graceful Astaire.

At the front in the ninepennies just past the rail,
The noise from the youngsters would rise up the scale,
Cricks in their necks looking up at the screen,
Which was too high above to be properly seen.

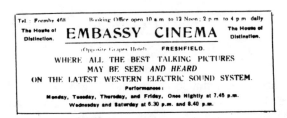

The interval lights would illumine the place,
And the girls would go out then to powder their face,
While the boyfriends would buy them an ice-cream or chocs,
Or a packet of fags and a Swan Vestas box.

If the film had been sad we would then mop our eyes,
Blow our noses and smile as we got up to rise,
And file down the aisles to get to the doors,
Where Jack Mawdsley was standing on duty of course.

We all loved the Embo and queued every night,
To see Hedy Lamarr or a good cowboy fight,
What a long time ago do those memories seem,
But it's only last week when you just sit and dream.

THE VILLAGE BOBBIES

They had no need for walkie-talkies,
No need at all for Panda cars,
Our bobbies here used Shanks's pony,
And never went to seminars.

No brass-hats breathing down their necks here,
No forms in triplicate to write,
Just leisured strolls around the village,
Keeping watch by day and night.

We knew them all and they knew us then,
Respected, held in high esteem,
These seven men were our protectors,
Reliable, trusted, first-rate team.

Then Formby was a quiet back-wash,
Open doors, no bolts and bars,
Crime was almost non-existent,
And hardly any motor cars.

Fred Beswick was the tall and lean one,
Small moustache and big flat feet,
We all felt safe with Fred amongst us,
Pounding round his Formby beat.

Norman Brooks, the quiet shy one,
Played piano in the band,
But don't forget he's still a copper,
Toe the line, or feel his hand!

Bob Greenhalgh was the big rotund chap,
Crime detection was his game,
Sergeant Coulthard at the station,
Watch your step—they knew your name!

George Davidson and big Bill Hoptroff
Were the men we all admired,
Plus P.C. Rooke, the mounted policeman,
All hoped they'd stay till they retired.

In such a law-abiding village,
Seven policemen seemed a lot,
But pay was low and no inflation
Meant the best was what we got.

Men of honour, poorly paid then,
Unsocial hours, but quite content,
Our Formby bobbies were our mentors,
And we missed them when they went.

F.U.D.C.

Once we had a district council,
Once we knew our place,
Once our chairman, Jimmy Rimmer,
Was a well known face.

Once we had our own officials,
Once we knew them all,
Once we used our Council Office
Like our own Town Hall.

Once when Harold Turner ordered,
Once they heard the shout,
Once our workmen knew their workload
They would all turn out.

Once Bob Sutton swept our roads clean,
Once our park was neat,
Once we had a thatched pavilion
Where we all could meet.

Once when John Breese was the king pin,
Once we knew the score,
Once when Formby was just Formby
We seemed to matter more.

Now we have no Formby council,
Now we've lost our way,
Now we're just a part of Sefton,
Completely gone astray.

THE LIBRARY SHOP
(LANCASHIRE COUNTY LIBRARY)

It was a wondrous place to be
When you were only just turned three,
And then when you were over four
The great delights were even more.
From five and six were better still,
So many things to cause a thrill.
Seven, eight, nine, ten, as minds awoke,
Came endless treasures for young folk,
For you could go there on your own,
Without your Mum or Dad—ALONE!
Where could this pleasure palace be?
The fairground, park, or by the sea?
Those venues all give real delight,
But only if the weather's right.
This paradise of endless joy
Was free to every girl and boy,
By READING you could live each word,
Be brave or clever, strong or scared.
Those days had no expansive hall,
Or endless stock for one and all,
A tiny shop supplied the need
Of those whose hobby was to read.

Despite its very modest size,
That library shop enthralled our eyes,
No lettered person with degree
Behind the desk in old Formby,
Just Mrs. Derbyshire in charge,
And literary wants were none too large,
She frightened us a little bit,
But then most grown-ups always did,
Her long black dress and glasses small
Perched on her nose to see us all.
How greatly things have changed today,
Technology now leads the way,
That tiny library shop has gone,
Replaced by a much grander one,
But it's so nice to think back when
How simple things were when you're ten.

THE MILK ROUND

Saturday morning,
Daylight was dawning,
Out of our beds we shot,
Down to the farm,
Peaceful and calm,
Where the horse waited ready to trot.

Each of us took turns,
Loading the milk churns
On to the old milk float,
Ladles were ready,
Dolly stood steady,
The reins loosely tied at her throat.

Bert Lawton was waiting,
And anticipating
How many children would be,
Bright-eyed but yawning,
At seven that morning,
Aboard for the ride that was free.

Riding the milk round,
Over the rough ground,
Bumping along with the horse,
This was like paradise,
Nothing could be so nice,
Heaven was like this of course.

Stop at each house gate,
Stagger with milk crate,
Down the front path to the door,
Fill up the milk jug,
Or the old pint mug,
Sometimes a tip was in store.

Back to the stable,
Ready and able
To unload the churns on the floor,
Into the dairy,
White-washed and airy,
The milk round was over once more.

This was the way then
We used to play when
The T.V. set hadn't been born,
Countrified pleasures,
Were our simple treasures,
Each Saturday morning at dawn.

THE BOAT HOUSE

In childhood days we never knew
The history of the lifeboat crew,
We didn't know we'd led the way
And launched a boat in Liverpool Bay.

To us the boat house was the shop
And cafe where we bought our pop,
Its sloping roof down to the shore,
And gaping massive wide front door.

Cold cobbles covered with blown sand
We walked upon, bare feet to stand
And change the bottles we had found
For copper pennies large and round.

A huge enclosure quite close by,
Beside the sea, beneath the sky,
Where all our bikes were in a stack,
Unlocked and safe till we came back.

The sea was clear, the shore was clean,
Hard ridges where the tide had been,
Wrecked boats and driftwood were our toys,
Sandhills resounding with our noise.

As setting sun joined sea and sky,
Back to the boat house we would fly,
Collect our bikes and ride away,
What perfect end to perfect day.

THE SWAMP

In winter months when snow lay deep,
And all of nature seemed asleep,
Down to the swamp we'd make our way,
And spend each frosty day at play.

The ice formed solid as a rock,
Dozens of children all would flock,
To slide and skid between the reeds,
Tentative steps to dizzy speeds.

No expert skaters; raw recruits,
No proper skates; just wellie boots,
We slipped and fell and staggered back,
Not caring if the ice should crack.

As winter's grip released its hold,
We bid goodbye to ice and cold,
The swamp returned to soggy slush,
With spiky reed and straight bullrush.

Now Gardner Road lies on the top
Of our dear swamp beyond Bull Cop,
Where gentle pussy willows grew,
When all the world to us was new.

ASPARAGUS

Down by the pines the asparagus grew,
A food much beloved by the affluent few,
In pure Formby sand by the edge of the sea
It was planted and grown, this delicacy.

Jimmy Lowe was acclaimed as Asparagus King,
His crops were world famous and bundles he'd bring
To sell in the village from humble small shops,
And transport on his lorries, these wonderful crops.

The gentry, the royals, all partook of his wares,
His daughters worked hard as the labours they shared,
Such lovely young girls slaving into the night,
In a season so short and a schedule so tight.

Just casual help and all hands to the pump,
A frantic work load before they could slump,
And know that their efforts were their own rewards,
In supplying this food to both princes and lords.

Formby asparagus was famed and renowned
Throughout all the country and it could be found
On fine royal plates and in great hallowed halls,
At society weddings and county hunt balls.

Lowe's asparagus fields can no longer be found,
No more feathery ferns in that poor barren ground,
As agricultural industry withered and died,
Pine Tree Farm disappeared with the incoming tide.

HARRINGTON BARRACKS

Hundreds of houses cloak the land
Where once the regiments did stand,
Young soldiers shattered from Dunkirk,
Back from a nightmare they'd not shirk.

In rags and tatters they were clad,
The lucky ones who were just glad
To have survived the beaches where
So many friends they'd left back there.

The peace of Formby's quiet lanes,
Stark contrast to the battle pains,
From bloody beach to silent shore,
These weary men were home once more.

Green beret and the khaki cap,
Where was this Formby on the map?
A place they'd never even heard,
Now here their billets they all shared.

Formby was teeming with the troops,
Marching feet and stamping boots,
Battalions line up on parade,
And children watching unafraid.

Exciting times for children's eyes,
Sweet innocence, a priceless prize,
Oblivious of the cruel war
That brought us sights unseen before.

Those soldiers left, a few returned
To make their homes and livings earned,
In this small village once unknown
They laid their roots and called it home.

The years passed by, the barracks died,
Fields, trees and flowers all expired
As houses sprang up smart and new
To change that lovely, rural view.

When we look back across the years,
When times were hard with many fears,
How could we ever visualize
That vast estate before our eyes?

Such natural beauty all around,
So many wild flowers to be found,
Now they're all gone and in their place
A homestead for the human race.

It had to be, it had to grow,
But we were lucky we could know
The way it was in times gone by,
When what we loved grew up to die.

V. J. NIGHT

Long trestle-tables down the middle of the road,
Sandwiches, jellies and cakes by the load,
Despite the food rations and those dreadful B.U.'s,
War was over at last—we knew we wouldn't lose.

Victory was celebrated all round the land,
And here in little Formby the parties were grand,
Great bonfires with To-Jo propped up on the tops,
And in the fields we were dancing amid the cow flops.

Union Jacks, lots of bunting—a wonderful scene,
Kids united with Dads they didn't know and hadn't seen,
Life was good once again, deprivation would be gone,
We could pick up the pieces and simply carry on.

The men and the boys who were lost in the war
Paid the ultimate price for our freedom once more,
Sadness and joy intertwined with relief
That a bright new tomorrow could be our belief.

When we sang and we danced back in 1945
The future looked good and hope very much alive,
Life went on, people prospered, the welfare state came,
Bringing apathy, greed, and nothing was the same.

Life today is much easier in very many ways,
But those dark days of Hitler seemed happier days,
When we all pulled together and did what we could
To help one another in a place that was good.

What's happened here in Formby is mirrored round the land,
Places grow, people change as progress is planned,
But did it need to change quite so dramatically,
That now we're just another place with no identity?

THE MARMALADE CART

Here we had no main drain sewerage,
Here the cess pool flowed,
And every Friday, early morning,
The chariot hit the road.

Here we had no sanitation,
Here the cockerel crowed,
And every Friday, early morning,
The chariot hit the road.

Here we had endangered species,
Here the natterjack toad,
And every Friday, early morning,
The chariot hit the road.

Here the bucket down the garden,
Here the candles glowed,
And every Friday, early morning,
The chariot hit the road.

Here was Hagan on the back seat,
Here to fetch the load,
And every Friday, early morning,
The chariot hit the road.

When we think of bygone Formby,
A picturesque abode,
Do we forget that every Friday
The muck cart hit the road?

THE WAR MEMORIAL

Armistice day,
Cloudy and grey,
The forces, the police on parade,
Processions so long,
The people would throng
In respect of the sacrifice made.

Fresh in the minds,
Memory finds
The time when those lost lives had been
The husbands and sons,
Destroyed by the guns,
In two wars that were wholly obscene.

Khaki and blue,
Everyone knew,
As they marched from the church to the cross,
With all civic heads,
To honour the dead
Of the wars that created such loss.

The cross stood erect,
A mark of respect,
In a corner of our village plot,
The names which it bore
Were with us no more,
For eternity now was their lot.

The memorial stands
On Weld Blundell land,
A gift to the villagers here,
That never shall we
Forget what we see,
And be grateful for all we hold dear.

A symbol of pride,
The shops alongside,
All their names, like the men, long since gone,
As we hurry on by,
Do we stop and think why
These young men were denied to live on?

They fought and they died
That we could abide
In an island of freedom and choice,
Though their Formby has gone,
Their names will live on,
Through their sacrifice we can rejoice.

Such growth and such change
Would today seem so strange
If those heroes returned from their rest,
For the Formby they knew,
With the fields wet with dew,
Has exploded like bombs in the west.

Estates now abound,
Where once was the ground,
A carpet of flowers and grass,
Let us never forget
That we all stand in debt
To those names etched in stone as we pass.

HOLY TRINITY

Our Church in Formby came to birth
In eighteen-eighty-nine,
She rose so proudly from the earth,
A symbol of love divine.

A monument from man to God,
A home for all to share,
The comfort of his staff and rod,
In-built with love and care.

A building to his glorious name,
A sanctuary of peace,
A haven where the faithful came,
And here their fears released.

Life's differing fortunes down the years,
The good times and the bad,
The jubilations and the fears,
Here shared, both warm and sad.

The evils of the first world war,
The dreadful bitter loss,
We shall remember evermore
Reminds the reredos.

The joy of marriage solemnized,
The miracle of birth,
The parting grief of sad demise
At journey's end on earth.

The wreathing and the gift of toys,
Mothering Sunday flowers,
The Easter eggs for girls and boys,
The harvest and God's powers.

The guides, the brownies, scouts and cubs,
The youth club and young wives,
The school, the bowling, tennis clubs,
All milestones in our lives.

An old yet ever youthful church,
All changing yet the same,
A loving, caring, hopeful church,
To the glory of God's name.

The choir stalls ringing with the sound
Of voices raised in praise,
Oh, Lord, we pray let grace abound
In all the coming days.

And may our Church live day by day
Into eternity,
That unborn congregations may
Bless Holy Trinity.

MRS. MITTON

A hundred years she lived and more,
In fact a hundred and four,
And in that time she left our shore—
The year nineteen-o-four.

She thought Australia would be fair,
And sailed away to sea,
But six months later she got there
And missed her old Formby.

Australia was a barren land,
So dusty and so hot,
She and her husband hand in hand,
Back on the ship they got.

Straight back to Formby they both came,
And opened up her shop
In Mitten's Lane—which took her name,
And there was glad to stop.

The smallest shop you'd ever find,
The best stock in the land,
So dark the kids could rob her blind,
But no— they'd all be banned.

This pokey little white-washed place
Was full of everything,
Tinned food and soap to wash your face,
Bread, cakes, and balls of string.

Potatoes, firewood, veg. and fruit,
Sweets, biscuits, matches, too,
Cinnamon sticks and liquorice root,
And paper for the loo.

Set in the fields in clean fresh air,
Right opposite the farm,
She'd never be a millionaire,
But could live in peace and calm.

No trace today of that small shop,
No sign of where she'd been,
No indication of the spot,
Which now is Smithy Green.

FORMBY HIGH

Amid the fields and ploughshares
This edifice appeared,
A blot upon the landscape,
But needed said our peers.

It housed the pre-war school kids
Who had nowhere else to go,
In a lovely brand new building
Looking like the Earls Court Show.

They came from Holy Trinity,
St Peter's and St. Luke's,
To start a new and different life,
With implements and books.

They'd never heard of science,
Bunsen burners full of gas,
Iron filings, blobs of mercury,
And Miss Parry head of class.

The boys were taught their woodwork,
And the girls to cook and sew,
Mr. Nelson was our idol,
And old Aggie scared us so.

The Browns brought out our culture
In both music and in art,
And sports and games were uppermost
And closest to the heart.

Blundell, Formby, Scarisbrick,
Were the houses of the school,
And sports day was the highlight,
Competition was the rule.

Now fifty years have passed away,
And new generations swot
A different type of learning
Than their forbears ever got.

More academic skills are taught,
Technology's the rule,
The education now required
Is light years from our school.

The school laid down the guide lines
Which set us on the track,
The rest was really down to us,
And now we can look back.

Just look around our Formby now,
With houses by the mile,
All built, maintained and serviced
By those kids from Formby High.

Good joiners, brickies, handy men,
Gardeners, plumbers, sparks,
They came in on the building boom,
And in business made their marks.

And so the school goes on today,
With kids who work and try
To emulate their parents
Who once went to Formby High.

MURIEL SIBLEY

We were so blind, we could not see
The things we loved and lost,
The cottages, then tree by tree
Into the past were tossed.

Our fields and lanes and ditches deep,
So slowly went away,
We shed no tears, we did not weep,
We lived just for the day.

Then into Formby came the one
Who saw what we could not,
Her bicycle she perched upon,
And with her camera shot
Each building as it bit the dust,
Each leafy lane that fell,
Her records captured for our trust,
The place we'd known so well.

With paint brush, film and artist's pen,
Such beauty she'd record,
Quite unappreciated then,
We locals would have scorned.

How could we know so long ago
How fortunate we were,
When Muriel came and said hello,
And stayed her life to share.

We owe so much to her today,
A precious record now,
Of how our lives were yesterday,
Mrs. Sibley take a bow.

DOCTOR TREE'S SURGERY

We know that coughs and sneezes
Will quickly spread diseases.
We know the things we're all supposed to eat.

We know that high cholestrol
Is like low octane petrol,
And makes our engines tick not quite so sweet.

We know that booze and nicotine
Are poison like the wicked queen
Laced in the apple for Snow White to eat.

We know that lack of exercise,
And sausage, bacon, eggs, and pies
Are full of things that really aren't a treat.

White flour and sugar too refined
Are foods we know that are defined
As just as bad as eating bright red meat.

And fruit and veg with pesticides,
Plus chicken and the rest besides
All narrow down the menu we can eat.

Salmonella and listeria
Cause some of us hysteria,
And fill the doctor's surgery each week.

So when we know all this today
Why do we still persist to say
We're here again to see our poor G.P?

The doctor's at our beck and call,
Why don't we just forget it all?
Then she'd be bored and have no one to treat.

Finally—
In this soccer mad mecca of Merseyside, and with the
changing climate of easy travel and the growth of Formby,
our own little football team has become completely over-
shadowed by the outstandingly successful first division teams
of Liverpool and Everton, with the familiar red and blue now
predominating over the orange and black of the past. The
tragedy of Hillsborough touched us all claiming the lives of
three of our young people and focusing the world's attention
upon us. Hillsborough is already part of our history.

HILLSBOROUGH

It's gear, it's fab, it's here again,
We're on the Wembley trail,
We'll slaughter Forest, Norwich, too,
We know we just can't fail.

Scouseland's going to win that Cup,
It's good as ours, we know,
The reds or blues, it's in the bag,
For Merseyside to show.

The whistle blew at Hillsborough's ground,
The crowds still pouring in,
All herded up and penned like sheep,
To see their heroes win.

The roars of scouse encouragement,
Rose loudly to the skies,
Come on you Reds, died on their lips,
As horror filled their eyes.

The surging crowds, the screams of pain,
The panic, and the fear,
The carnage as the buckled rails,
Left no escape from here.

Trapped in the snare like cornered rats,
The anguished cries rose up,
Of frantic souls in terror now,
Robbed of that Wembley Cup.

The devastation all around,
Such madness named as sport,
Young lives snuffed out when just begun,
Their tragic days cut short.

The game was stopped, the war was lost,
The troops condemned to die,
That peaceful Anfield army wrecked
Beneath the April sky.

The glory that was Liverpool,
The pride of Merseyside,
Lay lifeless on a battle field,
Whilst round them others cried.

No hooligans, no one to blame,
No lessons learned it seems,
First Ibrox, Bradford, and now this,
Are football's shattered dreams.

Is this the end? We've had so much,
Why us? the plea goes up,
Please God be with us in our need,
For Satan's claimed our Cup.

Surrounding design by David Mills

HILLSBOROUGH